ROCKS AND MINERALS

GET THE DIRT ON GEOLOGY

CHRIS EBOCH
Illustrated by Alexis Cornell

Nomad Press

A division of Nomad Communications

10 9 8 7 6 5 4 3 2 1

This book was manufactured by Versa Press, East Peoria, Illinois
January 2020, Job #J19-10190
ISBN Softcover: 978-1-61930-854-1
ISBN Hardcover: 978-1-61930-851-0

Educational Consultant, Marla Conn

Questions regarding the ordering of this book should be addressed to
Nomad Press
2456 Christian St., White River Junction, VT 05001
www.nomadpress.net

Printed in the United States.

Titles in the Inquire & Investigate
Earth Science set

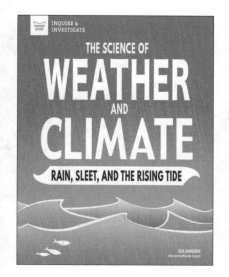

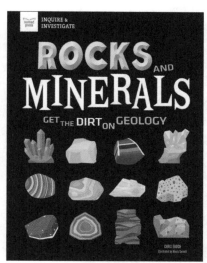

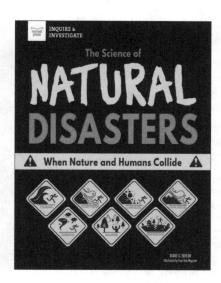

Check out more titles at www.nomadpress.net

You can use a smartphone or tablet app to scan the QR codes and explore more! Cover up neighboring QR codes to make sure you're scanning the right one. You can find a list of URLs on the Resources page.

If the QR code doesn't work, try searching the internet with the Keyword Prompts to find other helpful sources.

 rocks and minerals

What are source notes?

In this book, you'll find small numbers at the end of some paragraphs. These numbers indicate that you can find source notes for that section in the back of the book. Source notes tell readers where the writer got their information. This might be a news article, a book, or another kind of media. Source notes are a way to know that what you are reading is information that other people have verified. They can also lead you to more places where you can explore a topic that you're curious about!

Contents

TIMELINE

The timeline of Earth's lifespan is shown in a geologic timescale that is broken up into chunks of time called eras. Each era is made up of different periods. Some of the more recent periods are also divided into epochs. Check out the visual timeline on page 16.

4.54 billion years ago .... The earth forms.

4.4 billion years ago .... The oldest known minerals on Earth are formed.

3.5 to 3.9 billion years ago .... Life forms on Earth during the Archean eon.

200 to 250 million years ago .... Pangaea forms.

180 million years ago .... Pangaea breaks apart.

5 to 6 million years ago .... The Grand Canyon forms.

640,000 years ago .... The Yellowstone supervolcano explodes.

79 CE .... Mount Vesuvius in Italy erupts, completely burying the large Roman town of Pompeii.

c. 1076 .... A tsunami strikes southern China. The local civilization takes 500 years to recover.

1400s .... Leonardo da Vinci notes that a flood does not explain fossils embedded all the way through mountain rocks.

1768–1785 .... James Hutton develops some basic theories of geology.

1800s .... Geology becomes a scientific fad.

1815 .... A volcanic eruption in Indonesia kills 10,000 people directly and 80,000 more from famine.

1887................................. The first seismographs in the United States are installed in California.

1896................................. Radioactivity is discovered.

early 1900s........................ Seismology develops as a science.

April 18, 1906.................... An earthquake nearly wipes out San Francisco, California.

1908................................. The Lawson report gathers scientific information about the San Francisco earthquake, greatly increasing our understanding of earthquakes.

1915................................. Alfred Wegener publishes a book describing the theory of continental drift.

second half of the twentieth century .... The development of radiometric dating techniques allows geologists to determine the ages of rocks.

March 27, 1964 .... The largest recorded earthquake in the United States hits Prince William Sound, Alaska.

1968................................. The theory of continental drift is widely accepted.

1988................................. The United Nations forms the Intergovernmental Panel on Climate Change. The panel concludes that there is a more than 95-percent probability that human activities have warmed our planet.

December 26, 2004........... A tsunami in the Indian Ocean, triggered by an earthquake, kills more than 200,000 people.

March 11, 2011 .... A magnitude 9.0 earthquake hits Japan and sets off a tsunami that damages a nuclear power plant.

May 3, 2018...................... Lava starts flowing from the Kilauea volcano on the island of Hawaii, eventually destroying hundreds of homes and filling Kapoho Bay.

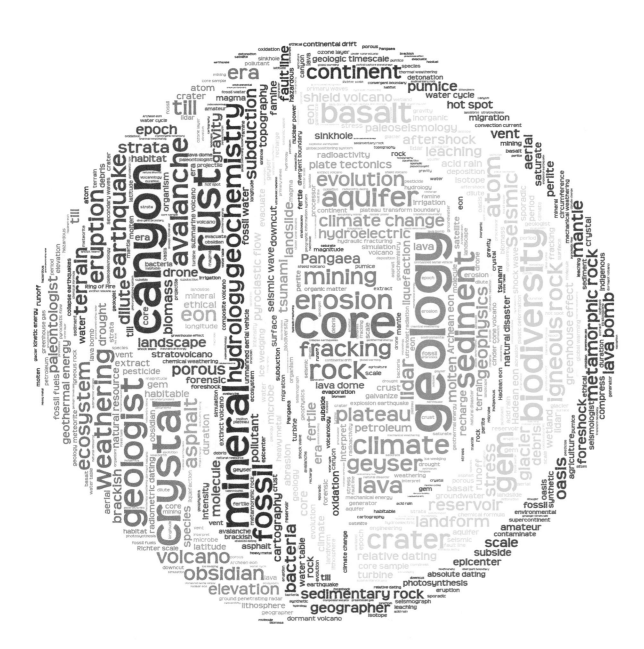

Understanding the Earth

WANNA KNOW WHY ROCKS ARE THE COOLEST EVER?

What do geologists do?

Geologists study the materials that make up the planet. They examine how those materials behave and what processes affect them.

● ● ● ● ● ● ● ● ●

Walk through a town or city, and you may notice the buildings, parks, sidewalks, and streets. Walk in the woods, and you might admire the trees and plants. But have you thought about what's happening under your feet? Geology is the study of the earth. Geologists study the earth to understand the history of our planet. They explore how the planet has changed through time.

If geologists understand the earth's past, they can better predict the future. That helps them improve our communities and even save lives!

Geologists work like detectives. They look for clues in the landscape on the surface of the earth. They look for clues under the earth's surface as well. It's not always easy to interpret these clues—rocks can't speak, though they can provide information. Geologists study the shapes of the land and examine evidence of erosion from water and air. They look for rocks, minerals, and the fossil remains of plants and animals.

Geologists working near Mount Etna in Italy, 2017

They may drill down to get samples from underground. Plus, geologists use special technology to make images of what's below the ground's surface.

Put together, the clues they find help scientists interpret what the land was like millions of years ago. In this way, geologists are better able to understand what is happening now and what may happen in the future.

VOCAB LAB

There is a lot of new vocabulary in this book. Turn to the glossary in the back when you come to a word you don't understand. Practice your new vocabulary in the VOCAB LAB activities in each chapter.

One reason geologists put so much effort into understanding how and why the earth behaves the way it does is because this knowledge can help save lives. Earthquakes, volcanic eruptions, floods, and landslides are all geologic processes. These natural disasters can be hazardous—even deadly—to people and other living things.

Geologists work to better understand these processes so they can offer advice to city planners. They can identify the areas most at risk of flooding or other hazards and can suggest avoiding building in the most dangerous areas. They can identify where special precautions should be taken to keep people safer.

Geologists are also working to predict natural disasters. If they can give people even a few minutes warning before an earthquake, thousands of lives could be saved. If they can accurately judge that a volcano is going to start spewing lava and ash, people will know when to evacuate.

Have you heard news reports about climate change? This is a global issue that is attracting more and more attention from scientists, the public, politicians, and businesses as the earth continues to warm.

Geologists are on the frontlines of the effort to understand climate change and figure out solutions to this problem.

They study how the climate of the earth has changed as eons have passed. Knowing the geological history of the planet helps us understand how our current climate is changing and what the future may hold.

TREASURES FROM THE EARTH

Geology helps people in many different ways. Have you ever heard the saying, "If it's not grown, it's mined?" That means if we can't grow a resource, we must extract it from the earth. Geologists find many of those resources.

How many of the earth's materials can you see from wherever you're sitting? Can you spot water, metal, and fabrics? Chances are good that you've got lots of the earth's resources in your sight.

Bingham Canyon copper mine southwest of Salt Lake City, Utah, in 1942. This mine is considered to have produced more copper than any other mine in history.

SCIENTIFIC METHOD

The scientific method is the process scientists use to ask questions and find answers. Keep a science journal to record your methods and observations during all the activities in this book. You can use a scientific method worksheet to keep your ideas and observations organized.

Question: What are we trying to find out? What problem are we trying to solve?

Research: What is already known about this topic?

Hypothesis: What do we think the answer will be?

Equipment: What supplies are we using?

Method: What procedure are we following?

Results: What happened and why?

ROCK SOLID

Geologists work in the field, mapping and taking samples. They work in labs, doing research. Some use computers to make models or maps. Geologists work for state or federal governments or private companies. Mining, engineering, and environmental groups all use geology.

A Close Look

Take a close look at a computer. Its plastic case is made from either gas or petroleum. The glass screen is mostly made of minerals. Inside, processors contain the mineral quartz, plus the metals copper and gold. Batteries contain more metals. Even the screws that hold everything together are made from metal. The vast majority of a computer is made possible because of materials found in the earth.

Many people depend on water pumped up from deep underground. Geologists can help find water and determine how to manage its use. Metals and minerals come from mines and are used in many different products. Large buildings use metal support beams. Metal is used in appliances, such as stoves and refrigerators, and in computers, cell phones, and other electronics.

Metals and minerals are even found in sunscreen, cosmetics, toothpaste, and soap. They are used in paper, printing inks, rubber, and some fabrics. Paint usually contains minerals and oils. Glass is made from sand heated to an extremely high temperature.

Oil, gas, and coal are more of Earth's resources pulled from underground. They are used to heat buildings and to generate electric power that's used for lights, televisions, microwaves, and much more. Petroleum products also power vehicles, from cars and buses to airplanes and trains. They are even used to make plastics, asphalt, and many fertilizers.

Many fabrics are also made from chemicals. These include stretchy Lycra, waterproof raincoats, and fluffy fleece. Without chemicals from the earth, we would still have natural fabrics such as cotton, silk, and wool—but synthetic fabrics can be more comfortable, stronger, and warmer or cooler.

> Our lives would be very different without the work of geologists!

Imagine your life without any of those things! No roads or bridges, buildings made only of wood with no glass windows, heat only from burning wood. No electricity for lights, no refrigerators and ovens, no computers or cell phones. Unless you have a stream or spring nearby, you wouldn't even have water.

Even NASA astronauts receive training in geology! This photo was taken in 1972.

credit: NASA

The earth goes through phases of warmer and cooler temperatures, but the last 100 years have seen a far faster increase in global temperature than ever before. You can watch a video showing average global temperatures at this website. Why does a warming planet cause so much concern?

 NASA warming trend

GEOLOGY TODAY

Geology can be divided into several branches, and geologists usually specialize in one of these branches. They might study earthquakes or volcanoes, help communities manage water resources, or decide where to build new housing developments. They could work for petroleum or mining companies to identify oil, natural gas, or minerals underground. Geologists are important to keeping our communities functioning and safe, and understanding the science of geology is valuable for everyone.

In *Rocks and Minerals: Get the Dirt on Geology*, you'll take on the role of geologist and learn how the earth formed and how it continues to change. Along the way, you'll have the chance to conduct experiments, build models, and explore the geology of your own community. Let's get started!

KEY QUESTIONS

- **What kinds of geological evidence can you spot in your community?**

- **Why is the study of geology important?**

- **How does understanding the past sometimes lead to understanding the future?**

INQUIRE & INVESTIGATE

Geology affects the landscape all around us. At first, it may seem that the landscape is hidden by buildings and other human artifacts. But take a closer look.

VOCAB LAB

Write down what you think each word means. What root words can you find to help you? What does the context of the word tell you?

climate change, **erosion**, **geology**, **mining**, and **resources**.

Compare your definitions with those of your friends or classmates. Did you all come up with the same meanings? Turn to the text and glossary if you need help.

- **Go into your community and look for different types of rocks.** How many can you find? Note stone walls, decorative rocks in yards, and sand in sandboxes. What about bricks or cement? What about plaster and roofing materials? How are they related to rocks?

- **Where did these materials come from?** Which rocks were taken from the ground in their current form? Which were altered by people? Research to find out how different materials are made.

- **Why might people choose different types of rocks or other building materials?** Compare rocks, metal, cement, bricks, and wood. What are the advantages and disadvantages of using each material?

To investigate more, research what natural hazards affect your community. Are you at risk of earthquakes or landslides? Are you close to a volcano that might erupt? Are you in a flood zone? How does the answer affect what building materials should be used locally?

Chapter 1

Earth on the Move: Plate Tectonics

DID YOU KNOW THE CONTINENTS ARE MOBILE?

How do we know about events that took place long before humans existed?

By studying rocks and minerals, geologists can determine when and how changes to the earth's surface occurred. Rocks are clues on a scientific treasure hunt!

● ● ● ● ● ● ● ●

Imagine you are an early human who comes upon a fossil embedded in the rock you're sitting on. How did it get there? Where did it come from? Questions such as these have driven the study of geology for centuries. Today's earth scientists are building on work done by other people for thousands of years.

For example, in ancient Greece, people wondered how rocks were formed. They were especially puzzled by the fossils they found. Why were there fossils of sea creatures in the high mountains when the ocean was nowhere to be seen?

The ancient Greeks came up with theories about erosion and how surface materials were deposited. They wrote descriptions of volcanic eruptions. But they had no way to test their theories. Now we know that many of their ideas were wrong, but the observations people made and recorded in ancient times were crucial to the understanding we have now.

BUT WHAT ABOUT . . .

It is surprising to find fossils of ocean creatures in the rocks of high, dry mountains. One popular early theory suggested that the gigantic flood described in a Bible story left the sea creatures up there, far from their natural habitat. But in the fifteenth century, Leonardo da Vinci (1452–1519) challenged that theory. He didn't think Noah's flood had anything to do with fossils.

Da Vinci is best known as an artist and inventor, but he was also a scientist. He applied the scientific method to questions he had about the earth and universe. He pointed out that a flood would deposit fossils only on the surface of the land. But fossils are embedded in the mountain rocks. How could those creatures have floated there in a flood? Noah's flood could not explain them!

Da Vinci suspected Noah's flood was not the right explanation for how fossils of sea creatures ended up in the mountains, yet he did not have an alternative explanation. One problem was that most people believed the earth was only 6,000 years old. If everything had formed in a few thousand years, the geology that people could see did not make sense.

In the eighteenth century, James Hutton (1726–1797) developed some of the basic theories of geology. Hutton was a doctor and farmer who studied the rocks around his home in Scotland. He hypothesized that some rocks formed through volcanic eruptions. Others formed when sand or clay eroded from higher areas. He also speculated that these processes were still continuing. He thought the earth was not formed 6,000 years ago in its present form. Instead, it was constantly changing.[1]

ROCK SOLID

Aristotle (384–322 BCE) was an ancient Greek philosopher and scientist. He thought volcanic eruptions and earthquakes were caused by violent winds coming from inside the earth.

James Hutton working in the field

FORGED IN FIRE

Many legends claim the world's beginning was fiery and chaotic. This is actually true! Billions of years ago, our solar system was merely a cloud of swirling dust particles. Then, gravity started pulling everything together and the sun became the center of the solar system. Other particles gathered into large, fiery balls of gas and molten liquid. They cooled and became solid, turning into the planets we know today.

ROCK SOLID

The first geology class was taught in 1775 at a small mining academy in Germany.

At the beginning of the nineteenth century, geology became a scientific craze. Professionals made charts of rock layers, naming them and determining when they were formed. Many amateurs got interested, too. After all, looking for fossils is fun! Both professional scientists and regular people helped deepen society's understanding of how the earth began.

CONTINENTS ON THE MOVE

Early geologists found plenty of clues about how the earth formed, but they had a harder time understanding the evidence. In addition to finding sea creature fossils on mountaintops, they found the same rock formations, with the same fossils, on different continents. How did these ancient animals get from one continent to another?

If you look at a map, you can see how the different continents fit together, like pieces of a puzzle. For example, the shorelines of Africa and South America could lock together. In fact, mountain ranges match up where the continents would meet. The Appalachian Mountains in the United States fit with the Caledonian Mountains in Scotland.

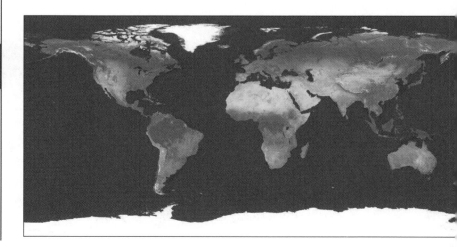

Rocks also match up by their type and age. Rock layers in South Africa match rock layers in Brazil. How could the same rock layers end up so far apart? It's as if someone tore a page of writing in two, and we can still read across the tear.

When glaciers move across a landscape, they reshape the land by carving away and sculpting some of the materials. They move massive amounts of broken rocks and soil debris. This activity leaves behind clear evidence that a glacier once existed.

Scientists found this evidence of ancient glaciers in surprising areas, such as southern Africa, where the climate is not suitable for glaciers. This suggests that the continents had once been connected, and had broken up and drifted to where they are now. This theory of "continental drift" was an important breakthrough that was finally widely accepted by 1968.

Today, scientists agree that the continents used to be one supercontinent known as Pangaea, which was formed roughly 200 to 250 million years ago. Later, the earth's crust fractured into rigid, moving plates.

Plate tectonics is the study of these plates and how they move.

As the plates move, they change the landscape. Where two plates push together, they create mountain ranges. The Himalayas, the highest mountains in the world, are still growing because two plates are still colliding. In other places, the plates are drifting farther apart. At these cracks, molten rock called magma wells up from inside the earth and solidifies into new land.

ROCK SOLID

Plate tectonics created mountains in the ocean. Some of these huge underwater mountain ranges are bigger than the Himalayas.

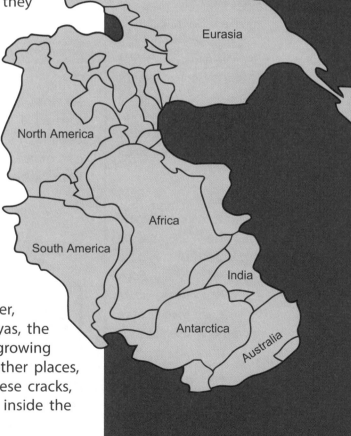

Eurasia

North America

Africa

South America

India

Antarctica

Australia

PUTTING THE PIECES TOGETHER

Alfred Wegener (1880–1930) was a world explorer who studied glaciers. He noticed that if you put the puzzle pieces of the continents together, ancient regional climates matched. In 1915, Wegener published a book suggesting the continents had been connected, broke up, and drifted to where they are now. Most scientists dismissed this idea. Wegener was a scientist, but not a geologist. Plus, he was German, and many people had anti-German feelings after World War I. Wegener's theory of continental drift wasn't widely accepted until 1968.[3]

Visit an online interactive world map to see what the world looked like during the last 750 million years. Enter your address to see where your home would have been in different eras.

 dinosaur pictures ancient earths

Technology developed in the last 50 years has provided evidence of plate tectonics, and new tools have identified the edges of these plates. Magnetic surveys of the ocean floor helped show the current boundaries of the plates underwater.[2]

FORMED IN FIRE

Now that we know the earth is billions of years old, the geology makes sense. In the beginning, the earth was much more geologically active. The first era of the earth's existence is called the Hadean eon. The planet was blisteringly hot, with intense volcanic activity. The surface was constantly bombarded by meteorites.

The name Hadean comes from the Greek word Hades, meaning "underworld."

As time passed, the surface of Earth cooled and formed a solid crust and oceans. As the planet cooled, heavier, denser material sank toward its center and lighter materials rose to the surface. Four layers of the planet developed.

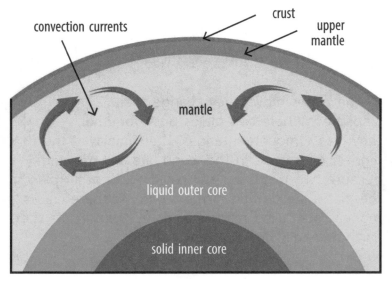

convection currents · crust · upper mantle · mantle · liquid outer core · solid inner core

The center of the earth, or the core, contains heavy metals.

The inner core is made of iron and nickel in a solid state. It is about 800 miles thick. The outer core is about 1,400 miles thick. It also contains iron and nickel, but in a liquid state.

The next layer is called the mantle. About 1,800 miles thick, this layer of rock contains silicon, iron, magnesium, aluminum, oxygen, and other minerals. In places it has the consistency of hot asphalt. It can move, but only very slowly.

The heat inside the earth creates convection currents. You may know that, above the earth, hot air rises, which pulls cooler air into its place. In a similar way, warm water rises in the ocean, while colder water sinks to the bottom. These forces create the weather on land and currents in the ocean.

Geologists believe that molten rock deep under the earth's surface also circulates by convection currents. Because this rock is in a semi-liquid state, it should behave like other fluids. The heat of the earth's core should cause the rock to become hotter and less dense, which would cause it to rise up from the bottom of the mantle. When it nears the cooler Earth's crust and loses heat, the rock becomes more dense and sinks back down to the core. This cycle is thought to help keep the earth's surface warm while contributing to the formation of earthquakes and volcanoes.

The solid, outer part of the earth is called the lithosphere. It includes the brittle upper portion of the mantle, along with the hard outer layer, the crust. Heat from the mantle below makes the rocks of the lithosphere more elastic, or able to deform under stress without breaking.

ROCK SOLID

The outer core may be 4000 to 9000 degrees Fahrenheit (2200 to 5000 degrees Celsius). That's so hot that all the metals are liquid. The inner core is equally hot. Yet it's under so much pressure that the metals are squeezed together into a solid.

Visit Incorporated Research Institutions for Seismology to learn about the lithosphere, convection currents, and other forces that drive plate tectonics.

 IRIS plate tectonics

THE LIGHT CRUST

The crust is made of the lightest materials. The rocks you find on the surface of the earth might seem heavy when you try to lift them, but they are far lighter than the heavy metals at the core. The crust is only 3 to 5 miles thick under the oceans, but on land, it can be about 25 miles thick. The crust is the best understood of all the layers. Why might this be?

ROCK SOLID

The temperature where the crust meets the mantle is about 1,600 degrees Fahrenheit (870 degrees Celsius). At that temperature, rocks begin to melt.

The lithosphere makes up the tectonic plates. Where tectonic plates shift apart from one another, the lithosphere is thinnest and may form deep valleys or ocean trenches. Sometimes, the plates slide past each other smoothly. At other times, they stick together and pressure builds up. As the pressure builds, the rocks bend—eventually, they may snap and break apart. We experience this as an earthquake. You will learn more about earthquakes in Chapter 3.

JUST ADD LIFE

Take a look at the geological timescale below. You can see that the Hadean eon ended roughly 3.8 billion years ago and the Archean eon began. This is another name taken from an ancient Greek word, meaning "beginning" or "origin." During this period, life forms began to evolve as the earth cooled.

The planet did not yet have oxygen, which most of today's life forms need. Nor did it have the ozone layer that protects us from the sun's damaging ultraviolet radiation. Still, life began to emerge in the form of microorganisms.

The geologic timescale, in millions of years ago

4,600	4,000	3,600	3,200	2,800	2,500	2,300	2,050	1,800	1,600	1,400	1,200	1,000	720	635	541.0	485.4	443.4	419.2

Hadean	Archean				Proterozoic										Phanerozoic			
	Eoarchean	Paleoarchean	Mesoarchean	Neoarchean	Paleoproterozoic				Mesoproterozoic			Neoproterozoi			Paleozoic			
FORMATION OF EARTH					Siderian	Rhyacian	Orosirian	Statherian	Calymmian	Ectasian	Stenian	Tonian	Cryogenian	Ediacaran	Cambrian	Ordovician	Silurian	Devonian
	Origin of Life														Age of Marine Invertebrates			Age of Fishes

During the Archean eon, the earth was much hotter than it is today. That made the planet much more geologically active. Tectonic plates moved faster—continents formed, moved, and broke up as the surface reshaped itself. Various supercontinents formed, broke apart, and recombined. The Archean eon lasted 1.5 billion years.

> Finally, sometime during the late Paleozoic and early Mesozoic eras, about 335 million years ago, the supercontinent we call Pangaea formed.

This most recent supercontinent broke apart 180 million years ago. After that, the continents drifted into the positions we know today. They carried the clues that they were once connected.

The first human ancestors appeared between 5 million and 7 million years ago. They began making crude stone tools by 2.5 million years ago. Our modern human species, *Homo sapiens*, likely evolved about 315,000 years ago. People began using land for agriculture around 12,000 years ago, and the first great civilizations began a mere 5,000 years ago. In geologic terms, 180 million years is the blink of an eye.

DID MINERALS MAKE LIFE?

Scientists are still refining their theories about how life arose. Some suggest minerals were important to the origin of life. The earliest life forms may have formed on mineral surfaces. As life evolved, minerals evolved as well. Today, new minerals are being formed through human activities. For example, some are forming from the waste products of mining activities. In landfills, the elements found in old computer screens are combining into new minerals. In fact, 30 to 50 new minerals are discovered every year!

	252.2	201.3	145.0	66.0	23.0	2.6	Today	
								EONS
		Mesozoic			Cenozoic			**ERA**
Permian	Triassic	Jurassic	Cretaceous		Paleogene	Neogene	Quaternary	**PERIOD**
ans	Age of Reptiles				Age of Mammals			

TASTE THE FORMULA

Most minerals can be described with a chemical formula. Do you put salt on your mashed potatoes? You're using the mineral NaCl! Each molecule of salt consists of one sodium atom (Na) and one chlorine atom (Cl). Some minerals have very complicated formulas, with many different parts. A few consist of only one type of atom. But if you change any part of the chemical formula, you have a different mineral.

ROCK SOLID

A few rocks don't quite fit the scientific definition of a rock. Mercury becomes solid if it is cold enough, but it is not solid at normal temperatures. Coal is often considered a rock, but it comes from plant matter.

An understanding of geologic periods led to a better, more complete understanding of the earth's history. People added to that knowledge through the study of fossilized animals and plants. Learning how animals and plants changed during thousands of years led to the theory of evolution. But it all started with rocks.[4]

ROCKS AND MINERALS

Rocks are the most common material on Earth—they make up the earth's crust and are easy to find on the surface of the land! But what exactly are rocks?

A rock is a naturally occurring solid made up of minerals. The word *mineral* is sometimes used for any substance that is neither vegetable nor animal, but the scientific definition is a little trickier. A mineral is an inorganic substance, meaning it is not alive and has never been alive. It is a solid that forms naturally. Every type of mineral has a distinct crystal structure and a specific chemical composition, both of which are always the same for that mineral.

Some rocks are made of a single mineral. For example, quartz is a rock made from the mineral quartz. Marble consists of a single mineral called calcite.

Most rocks are mixtures of several minerals. Do you have granite countertops in your kitchen? Granite is a very common rock that contains quartz, mica, feldspar, and other minerals. When rocks are made of several different minerals, they mix together like the ingredients of a salad—the individual minerals can still be identified, just as you can still see the individual pieces of lettuce, tomato, and carrot.

Most minerals form only under certain conditions. That means if we can identify the minerals in a rock, we can learn more about that rock, possibly even where and when it was formed.

Some minerals form when magma erupts out of a volcano and then cools. Some form deep within the earth's crust as a result of enormous heat and pressure. Some form through evaporation on the surface of the earth. All of this means that rocks carry the clues to their origin.

For example, in the Hawaiian Islands, a material called basalt erupts out of volcanoes. Basalt contains a mineral called olivine, which typically forms within the earth's mantle. It comes from depths greater than 43 miles.

> This tells us that the magma that forms the Hawaiian Islands comes from very deep underground.

Scientists can also use an understanding of mineral formation to find valuable resources. Precious gems, such as diamonds, are found in certain rock formations. Minerals used in industry may be found in other formations. Some geologists work for corporations that want to find more of these valuable resources.

THE TROUBLE WITH DEFINITIONS

People sometimes use the words rocks, minerals, and metals in different ways. That's partly because scientists tend to need more precise definitions than nonscientists do. Also, these words have been around for a long time, and meanings can change. At first, scientists didn't have a way to examine the chemical composition of minerals. Minerals were described according to qualities, such as their shape and hardness. Later, scientific advances allowed more accurate descriptions, and some terms changed.

Basalt rock formations

THE ROCK CYCLE

The earth has about 3,800 different kinds of minerals. But all rocks are divided into just three major groups! These are igneous, metamorphic, and sedimentary rocks. The names describe how they were formed. Let's take a closer look.

Remember magma, the molten rock inside the earth? Magma is molten because it is so hot, but as magma moves upward to cooler regions of the earth, it loses heat. The magma cools and crystallizes, becoming igneous rock. This can happen under the earth's surface, as magma moves upward in the crust layer, or magma can erupt from a volcano and then cool. Magma contains eight common elements, so these elements make up most igneous rocks.

ROCK SOLID

The oldest known minerals on Earth are zircons, found in Australia. They date back to almost 4.4 billion years.

Metamorphic rock in the Rocky Mountains, surrounding a seam of granite

credit: James St. John (CC BY 2.0)

Metamorphic rocks are formed at high temperatures and pressure. These cause the minerals in the rock to become unstable—they may form into larger crystals, form new minerals, or reorient themselves into layers. And they do this without melting.

Geologists can learn a lot from metamorphic rocks. They can tell what kind of temperature and pressure formed the rock based on the mineral and crystal structures. They can also infer the original type of rock, before it changed. All this helps them understand the geological history of an area.

Sedimentary rocks are formed from broken pieces of other rocks.

Rocks are tough, but a process called weathering can break them down into smaller parts, called sediment. Weathering is usually caused by wind, rain, or water that freezes and breaks apart rocks. The sediment might move to new places, carried by the wind, flowing water, or even gravity.

Eventually, sediments are put down in one place in a process called deposition. As layers build up, the weight of the sediments squeezes all the particles together. Dissolved minerals may fill in the spaces and cement these particles in place—and new sedimentary rock is created. Sedimentary rocks may also be formed from dissolved chemicals that turn solid. As water evaporates, it can leave behind deposits that crystallize into solid rocks.

Metamorphosis refers to a change in form, structure, substance, or appearance.

● ● ● ● ● ● ● ● ●

Sedimentary rock
credit: James St. John (CC BY 2.0)

Have you ever found a fossil in a rock? That's sedimentary rock. Sedimentary rocks sometimes contain fossils of the animals and plants that lived on Earth millions of years ago. They hold clues about what the earth's surface was like in the geologic past. Sedimentary rocks may contain reservoirs of drinking water or deposits of oil and gas.

Geologists are sometimes able to identify types of rocks by sight. Sandstone, a sedimentary rock, shows layers from the different sediments that settled. Its grains are rounded from weathering. On the other hand, granite is an igneous rock, so it shows no layering. It has a rough texture with sharp-edged crystals that have not been rounded by weathering. You may be able to identify the different minerals by their colors.[5]

Igneous rock

Some rocks on Earth are billions of years old. And rocks are constantly being reformed. Igneous, sedimentary, or metamorphic rock can be buried deep in the earth. There, with enough heat and pressure, the rocks might be transformed into new metamorphic rock. Meanwhile, rocks that melt can become new igneous rocks.

If rocks are exposed at the earth's surface, weathering can break them down. If those particles come to rest somewhere and combine into hard rock, that new rock is sedimentary. Any type of rock can become another type of rock. The rock cycle continues!

Many of the earth's processes are well understood today, but geologists are still making new discoveries. They are getting closer to answering some of the most important geological questions. For example, they would like to know how to predict, and perhaps someday even control, earthquakes and volcanoes.

KEY QUESTIONS

- **How did fossils provide clues to how the earth was formed?**

- **When was the theory of plate tectonics developed? Why did it take so long for people to accept it as a possibility?**

- **How does geology lead to other areas of scientific study?**

VOCAB LAB

Write down what you think each word means. What root words can you find to help you? What does the context of the word tell you?

continent, convection current, igneous rock, lithosphere, metamorphic rock, mineral, plate tectonics, and sedimentary rock.

Compare your definitions with those of your friends or classmates. Did you all come up with the same meanings? Turn to the text and glossary if you need help.

Text-to-World Connection

● ● ● ● ● ● ● ●

Have you ever had a rock collection? What kinds of rocks did you collect?

THE GEOLOGIC TIMESCALE

We usually measure time in years, days, hours, and minutes. Geologists need to measure the earth's entire 4.54-billion-year history! The geologic timescale is the calendar of events in the planet's history. It divides all that time into units called eons, eras, periods, epochs, and ages. These time units match the earth's rock formations.

To investigate more, become a rock hound. A rock hound collects rocks, minerals, and fossils. Explore your area and collect rocks where it is legal to do so. Check the laws for rock hounding in your state. In most cases, except for national parks and national monuments, public lands are open to rock hounding— but you cannot collect historical artifacts or fossils from vertebrates. And, sometimes, you need a permit. See if you can identify the types of rocks you find.

A natural history museum is a great place to see more rocks. Also, visit these sites for more information!

mindat

Friends of Mineralogy

- **Research the geologic timescale and examine the chart on page 16.** Then, make your own toilet paper geologic timescale. This will help you visualize the immense time in question.

- **Take a roll of toilet paper with at least 5,000 squares.** Each square of toilet paper represents 1 million years of the earth's history.

- **On the first square, mark the age of humans.** Recorded human history has lasted about 10,000 years, or $\frac{1}{100}$th of a square. Our species has been around for about 50,000 years, or $\frac{1}{20}$th of a square.

- **Start unrolling the toilet paper.** You could put a pencil or stick through the roll's tube and have a partner gently pull on the loose end to unwind it. If the paper rips, tape it back together.

- **As the toilet paper unrolls, count the squares and match them to the eons and eras on the geologic timescale.** Lay the paper along the ground, circling the room if necessary.

- **Go back to the first square.** How far away are the dinosaurs? How far away are the Hadean eon and the Archean eon? What does this tell you about geologic time?

Chapter 2 ▷
Volcanoes Ooze, Sputter, and Blow

What role do volcanoes play in the formation of land?

As magma erupts from beneath the earth's crust, it flows outward and eventually hardens as it cools completely.

• • • • • • • •

Many of the earth's geologic forces are hidden underground—or they move so slowly that we can't see them in action. Volcanoes, however, are another matter. They demonstrate the active power of the earth—sometimes explosively.

Volcanoes are fascinating to many people. In 2018, lava started flowing on the island of Hawaii. In a few days, it destroyed hundreds of homes. Lava filled Kapoho Bay, a place where visitors and locals swam and snorkeled. Many people gathered to watch lava flow into the bay. Boats even carried tourists who were eager to see lava glowing with orange fire and hissing as it touched the water. As deadly as volcanoes can be, they are also beautiful.

WHAT CAUSES VOLCANOES?

Magma, the molten rock inside the earth, usually stays under the earth's crust. But, in some places, an opening on the surface allows magma to escape, which results in a magma eruption—a volcano!

Magma reaches the earth's surface in three different ways. When tectonic plates slowly move away from each other, magma rises to fill in the space. This can cause volcanoes to form, even underwater. Magma also rises when tectonic plates move toward each other. When plates collide, part of the earth's crust may be forced down into the interior. This crust can melt under the high heat and pressure of the earth's interior, and rise as magma. Finally, magma can rise through hotspots, which are areas inside the earth that are especially hot.

> If magma reaches the earth's surface in any of these ways, it can form a volcano.

Once magma reaches the surface of the planet, it's called lava. Some volcanic eruptions are explosive, shooting material into the sky. In other eruptions, the magma flows gently. Volcanoes sometimes also release ash, cinders, and gas.

 See a short video from the U.S. Geological Survey (USGS) of lava flowing into Kapoho Bay.

🔍 USGS video
Kīlauea Volcano

LAVA BOMB!

Even a quiet volcano can throw out objects called "lava bombs." Also called volcano bombs, these are cooling blobs of molten lava that the volcano has spit out, which partly or entirely solidify as they come down. These balls can be anywhere from 2½ inches to 20 feet in diameter and they can do terrible damage. Some early Europeans thought lava bombs were spirits. The bombs often hissed as they flew through cooler air—people thought this sound came from souls screaming in pain. During the 2018 volcanic eruption in Hawaii, a lava bomb the size of a basketball hit a tour boat. It smashed through the roof and injured 23 people. Another lava bomb hit a man standing on a balcony. The bomb splintered his lower leg and knocked him onto a couch, which then caught fire. Volcanoes aren't the safest things to view up close!

Tuvurvur volcano in Papua New Guinea—a cinder cone volcano
credit: Taro Taylor (CC BY 2.0)

TYPES OF VOLCANOES

Geologists divide volcanoes into four types, depending on how they form. Cinder cone volcanoes are recognizable by their cone shape. They build up when blobs of lava and ash particles are ejected from a single volcanic vent.

As the ash explodes into the air, it breaks into small fragments that fall as cinders. The pieces rain down around the vent, and as time passes, a circular or oval-shaped cone builds up. Cinder cone volcanoes typically don't rise more than about 1,000 feet, and most have a bowl-shaped crater at the summit.

Crater Lake in Oregon, at the top of a composite volcano

See a video of a geologist sampling lava at an active volcano. Why do scientists take risks such as this?

 Insider geologists sample volcanoes

Mauna Loa, a shield volcano
credit: kanu101 (CC BY 2.0)

Composite volcanoes, also called stratovolcanoes, have an internal system that channels magna from deep within the earth to the surface. They often have a crater at the summit, plus lava may break through walls or fissures on the sides of the mountain. These volcanoes can form up to 8,000 feet tall and explode violently. Mount Fuji in Japan and Mount Rainier and Mount Saint Helens in the state of Washington are famous composite volcanoes.

Shield volcanoes are large and broad—they look like shields from above. Out of these pours thin lava that can travel for long distances down the shallow slopes of the volcano. These volcanoes build up slowly, with hundreds of eruptions creating many layers, so they seldom explode violently.

The Hawaiian Islands are a series of shield volcanoes that include Mauna Loa, the world's largest active volcano. It rises 28,000 feet from its base on the ocean floor, including 13,677 feet of land above sea level.

ROCK SOLID

Mountains can form without volcanic activity. Colliding tectonic plates can push sections of the earth's crust upward. Rocks on one side of a fault—a crack in the earth's crust where tectonic plates move against each other—may rise higher than on the other side. Erosion can also wear away the landscape, leaving mountains behind.

VOLCANOES OOZE, SPUTTER, AND BLOW

29

Finally, lava domes are created by thick lava that can't flow very far. The material may build up underneath the ground, or lava may pile up around a vent. A large composite volcano may have hundreds of lava domes across its sides or within its crater. Lava domes tend to build up with steep sides and rough surfaces. They can explode violently, as Mont Pelee in Martinique did in 1902, killing 30,000 people with fast-moving ash flows and poisonous gases.

While volcanoes can be deadly, volcanic activity created the earth's surface. Fortunately, many ancient volcanoes are now dormant or extinct.

A lava dome on Kilauea Big Island, Hawaii

credit: incidencematrix (CC BY 2.0)

Volcanoes are considered extinct if they are unlikely to erupt again. Dormant volcanoes might erupt at some time in the distant future, but are not currently active.[6]

DANGER!

People fear volcanic eruptions for a reason. When lava flows gently, instead of exploding, people have time to escape. But mixtures of hot gas and ash, called pyroclastic flows, can race down the slopes of volcanoes at 60 to 125 miles per hour! They are hot, choking, deadly, and impossible to outrun.

Even if you do escape the pyroclastic flow, there are other dangers. Volcanoes release gases into the air. The most common gas, water vapor, does not cause many problems. More harmful gases are released in smaller amounts and are quickly diluted as they mix with the air. Still, these can be dangerous for people with breathing problems.

> The ash released by volcanoes can cause trouble both near and far.

In 1815, the eruption of Mount Tambora in Indonesia killed 10,000 people. Then, volcanic ash destroyed crops and 80,000 more people died from famine. In fact, 1816 was known as the "year without summer" across the Northern Hemisphere, because the climate around the world was affected by the amount of ash in the atmosphere.

Volcanoes can also cause avalanches and landslides. They can set off tsunamis, which can devastate coastlines. People who live near a volcano that erupts may have to abandon their homes forever.[7]

EAST AND WEST

The eastern United States is no longer volcanically active. It has no plate boundaries or hotspots that would allow magma to escape. That could change some day, but it will take hundreds of millions of years! On the other hand, the west coast of the United States has several active volcanoes.

ROCK SOLID

Because ash travels on air currents, it can affect nearby cities differently. One city might be fine, while another city farther away is destroyed.

READY TO BLOW?

Our planet's land surface holds about 1,500 potentially active volcanoes. Active volcanoes include those that have erupted in the past 10,000 years. About 500 have erupted in historical time, so we have written records of these. Others have not erupted in centuries, but they are still capable of eruption. That is why they are called potentially active. Indonesia has the most volcanoes that have been active in historical times, followed by Japan. The United States is third. Roughly 1,500 more volcanoes in the United States have erupted in the past 10,000 years. However, these are not likely to erupt again in our lifetimes. Still, the United States has 169 potentially active volcanoes. Of these, 18 volcanoes are considered "high threat." Eleven of these are in Washington, Oregon, and California. Five are in Alaska and two are in Hawaii. All of these volcanoes are near large population centers or below busy air traffic corridors. They are also explosive volcanoes that could send projectiles long distances.[8]

Volcanic ash erupting from Mount Cleveland in Alaska

credit: NASA

The Hawaiian goddess Pelehonuamea, also called Pele, is the goddess of fire and volcanoes. She is known to devour the land with molten lava, which creates new land in the process.

Any erupting volcano can cause harm—the degree of danger depends on the type of eruption. Remember, a slow magma flow allows people time to escape, while a sudden, explosive eruption will typically do more damage.

The volcano's location also affects its potential for danger. A volcano in a remote area might cause little damage to people even during a huge eruption, but a smaller eruption near several large cities could be devastating.

Even a volcano considered to be a moderate threat could have worldwide effects. As we've discussed, an exploding volcano can release huge clouds of ash. Microscopic particles of volcanic rock can clog engines, which is hazardous to airplanes.

Most volcanic eruptions affect areas with light air traffic, and planes can simply be rerouted around any ash clouds. But that wasn't possible in the spring of 2010, when the Eyjafjallajökull Volcano erupted in Iceland. The resulting ash cloud covered much of Europe and reached several miles into the air. Many countries closed their airspace to any travel for several days. Thousands of travelers were stranded and could not get home.

Experts scrambled to respond to the crisis. They took samples of the ash and tracked the ash cloud in order to better understand how it would affect airplanes. Finally, experts declared the air to be safe and planes were able to fly again.

The Eyjafjallajökull eruption was not even especially large. How will people handle a much larger one? Scientists are learning from past experiences to prepare for the next eruption.

> Geologists can help predict which volcanoes will erupt and when. They advise the authorities on when to recommend an evacuation.

In the United States, the U.S. Geological Survey (USGS) has a program to monitor volcano hazards. The organization constantly watches volcanic activity and conducts research. The information it provides can help with planning for emergencies, including warning people to evacuate.

The effects of a volcano can last for thousands of years. Lava cools into fields of hard, rough, black basalt. A lava field can extend for thousands of square miles. This creates an otherworldly landscape that many tourists are drawn to, such as Valley of Fires in New Mexico, or Hell's Half Acre and Craters of the Moon Lava Field, both in Idaho.

Visit the Melbourne Museum to see an expert explain why some volcanoes erupt gently and others explosively.

 Melbourne eruption different volcano

UNDERSEA VOLCANOES

Seventy-five percent of all volcanic activity on Earth takes place in the ocean. The ocean floor holds too many volcanoes to count. Some 75,000 of them rise more than half a mile above the ocean floor. More than 450 volcanoes are located along the Ring of Fire, a large area in the Pacific Ocean where many tectonic plates overlap. Even underwater volcanoes can affect the land by causing tsunamis or releasing heat and chemicals into the ocean. Scientists are still learning about these submarine volcanoes.

Learn how NASA and other agencies around the world track volcanic clouds and issue alerts.

 NASA safer skies

VOLCANO TOURISM

Volcanoes shaped the Yellowstone Plateau in Wyoming. Three massive volcanic explosions hit the area in the past 2.2 million years. The most recent was 640,000 years ago, and smaller events continued up to 70,000 years ago. This activity left behind hot springs and geysers, such as the legendary Old Faithful. Millions of tourists visit Yellowstone National Park to see the geysers erupt. The park is an active volcano and is closely monitored for activity, but tourists are still able to enjoy the natural beauty and wonder that can be found there!

Scientists in Hawaii have even used the Kilauea volcano for fieldwork, because it has some similarities to the surface of Mars. The Kilauea lava fields are younger than the basalt rocks on Mars, but they may help scientists learn how life could have developed and survived on Mars.

As time passes, rainfall breaks down the rock into soil. Pockets in the basalt collect dirt and seeds that blow in on the wind. Plants grow. Eventually, you will no longer be able to see the lava flow. Depending on the rainfall and other factors, this process can take a few years or thousands of years.

WHY WE NEED VOLCANOES

Volcanoes can cause a lot of damage, yet early people often settled near volcanoes, and for good reason. When volcanoes erupt, ash can spread over a wide area. The makeup of the ash varies, but it typically contains chemicals that are healthy for the soil.

That means the mountain slopes and valleys near volcanoes are usually very fertile and terrific for growing crops. Some of the best farmland in the world owes its productivity to ancient volcanoes.

Volcanic activity also creates new land. Many island chains were created by volcanic eruptions. This is true of islands throughout the Pacific Ocean, including the Hawaiian Islands. Early travelers used these islands as rest stops during long sea journeys. People also settled there, growing crops on the ash-enriched slopes.

Today, the land close to volcanoes is often cheap and the scenery is beautiful. For some people, that's worth taking a chance on losing their homes to lava.

Eruptions produce useful types of rocks as well. People mine pumice, which is volcanic rock, and perlite, or volcanic glass. Because they are lightweight, pumice and perlite make good building materials. They are used in everything from roofs to plaster to highway blacktop to cement. Pumice is also gritty, so it is used as an abrasive to scrape and polish surfaces or added to soaps and cleansers.

Obsidian, a volcanic glass, breaks in a way that leaves sharp edges. During the Stone Age, people used it for arrowheads, spear points, and cutting tools.

Today, obsidian is sometimes used for surgical equipment. The cutting edge of obsidian is many times finer than the best steel scalpels, which means tissue cut with obsidian might heal faster with less scarring.

Listen to a volcano scientist describe his job with the USGS. Does this sound like a career you'd like to have?

 USGS seismologist job

ROCK SOLID

The word *geothermal* comes from "geo," which refers to the earth, and "thermal," relating to heat.

Volcanoes are even a source of useful metals and precious gems. Metals from volcanoes are used in electronics, machinery, and medicine. Stones such as opals, fire agates, and onyx make beautiful jewelry.[9]

ENERGY FROM THE EARTH

Volcanoes are a source of enormous heat, which is a form of energy. As magma comes closer to the surface, it heats any underground water. This hot water may become hot springs or geysers. Even dormant volcanoes can be surrounded by these hot springs.

Geysers, boiling mud pools, and hot springs attract tourists, bringing money into a volcanic region. Plus, these features are more than just fun to look at or good to soak in. The earth's heat can be harnessed for geothermal energy.

Electricity can be produced in several ways. A common method starts with coal or gas. These products are burned to create steam, which spins the large blades of a turbine engine. That spinning converts the heat energy into movement, or kinetic energy. An attached generator converts the kinetic energy into electrical energy, which can light our homes and power our appliances and devices.

Geothermal power uses the heat from inside the earth to create steam to turn the blades of a turbine. This is a cleaner way of producing energy, and it can be cheaper than using coal or gas. Burning coal, natural gas, or oil releases pollution and contributes to the high level of carbon dioxide in the atmosphere.

PRESERVED IN ASH

In 79 CE, Mount Vesuvius in Italy suddenly erupted. Volcanic ash completely buried the large Roman town of Pompeii, killing many people. The town was excavated in the nineteenth and twentieth centuries, when archaeologists uncovered buildings, statues, household goods, and skeletal remains. They made plaster casts of the impressions left by dead people buried in ash. These finds allowed archaeologists to reconstruct the daily life of the town from 2,000 years ago.

Geothermal power plants produce far fewer polluting gases. Plus, geothermal energy is a renewable resource. This means it will not run out, as coal and oil will eventually.

Hot water can be pumped from the ground, the heat extracted from it, and the water pumped back down. Then, the water picks up more heat so it can be used again. Geothermal energy is an environmentally friendly, efficient-energy source. Geologists can help energy companies find geothermal resources and make the best use of them.

The 1973 lava flow on the island of Heimaey in Iceland

credit: Urbain J. Kinet

WHERE IN THE WORLD

Geothermal power produces a large percentage of the power supply for some countries. Kenya, Iceland, New Zealand, and the Philippines all use a lot of geothermal power. What else do they have in common? Active volcanic regions! The western United States also has areas suited to geothermal power. Klamath Falls, Oregon, sits on natural hot springs. The city has 600 geothermal wells, which heat homes, schools, and a hospital. A power plant converts some of the energy into electricity. Hot water is even piped under the roads and sidewalks to melt snow. Dozens of other U.S. communities could make use of geothermal power. As people demand energy sources that help alleviate the problem of climate change, geothermal power plants could pop up in more and more places.

HOLDING BACK THE LAVA

Wouldn't it be nice if we could get the benefits of volcanoes without the dangers? People have tried some wild things to stop or control volcanic activity. For example, in 1935, the Hawaiian volcano Mauna Loa erupted, sending lava flowing toward the city of Hilo. Scientists and the U.S. Army developed a plan to alter the lava's direction.

Ten Air Force bombers dropped 20 bombs onto the exposed lava in the hope that the craters would divert the lava. Most of the bombs missed, though five bombs landed directly in the flowing lava. They blasted big craters, which quickly filled up, and the lava kept going.

> Lava can flow up to 40 miles per hour and can keep flowing for months or even years.

Fortunately, Mauna Loa stopped erupting several days later. The lava never reached Hilo, but that was more a matter of luck than due to human intervention.

Lava flows can be partly moved, sometimes. Just like water, flowing lava looks for the easiest path downhill. People have built rock walls to stop the lava and roads to direct the flow in a certain direction. This helped initially in two Hawaiian eruptions in 1955 and 1960. However, the lava quickly overwhelmed the barriers.

Iceland tried a different tactic in 1973. Lava was flowing toward the nation's most valuable fishing port. The country began pumping up ocean water and blasting it onto the front of the lava flow, cooling it enough so the lava solidified.

People worked for five months and used 1.5 billion gallons of ocean water. Iceland still lost part of the town, but the harbor was saved.

One challenge with diverting lava is determining where to send it. In 1669, Italy's Mount Etna threatened the town of Catania. The townspeople cut through a natural ridge to divert the lava flow. It worked, but the lava headed for another town! The residents of Paterno were not happy about that. They stopped the people of Catania from keeping the new path clear, and when the path clogged, lava swept through Catania.

That's one of the challenges of changing a lava flow. Who gets to decide where it goes? Even setting aside that ethical question, it's almost impossible to stop lava.

> When Iceland saved its harbor,
> the lava was flowing very slowly,
> which gave people time to make
> a plan and carry it out.

Sometimes, lava flows quickly, and its path can be unpredictable. Lava is dense and heavy and can reach temperatures of more than 1,800 degrees Fahrenheit (2,000 degrees Celsius). That's hot enough to destroy almost anything it touches.

In some cases, barriers and trenches have helped keep lava from reaching buildings. But their use is limited. They might divert just enough lava to save a town—if the volcano stops erupting in time. Most geologists think that trying to divert lava is pointless. Geologists can still help, however, by warning people of the hazards of volcanoes and recommending evacuations.

VOLCANOLOGISTS

What would you do if a volcano erupted near you? Most people would flee, but some scientists get closer. They risk intense heat, poisonous gases, choking ash clouds, and boiling floods of mud. They might even have to dodge lava bombs shooting through the air like missiles.

The study of volcanoes is called volcanology, and it is considered a branch of geology. Volcanologists have one of the most dangerous jobs in science. They have died from falls, helicopter crashes, and being hit by lava bombs. Even when studying an inactive volcano, the work of volcanologists is not easy. They might live in tents for two or three months of every year.

Text-to-World Connection

● ● ● ● ● ● ●

Would you choose to live near a volcano, knowing the dangers and benefits?

See a video from National Geographic on volcanologists working in the field.

 Nat Geo volcanologist

They spend their days walking rough terrain taking notes and photographs, collecting samples, and making sketches. They analyze samples in the lab to make sense of what they found and use computers to understand the information and write reports.

Not all volcanologists risk their lives at the edges of volcanoes. Some study volcanoes from a distance. They can take the volcano's temperature with a camera on a helicopter, airplane, or satellite. They can make 3-D maps and measure ground movements. They might study the chemicals in gases released by volcanoes.

It's a challenging life, yet volcanologists may travel to beautiful places, such as Hawaii or Antarctica. Many enjoy working outdoors. Plus, their research advances science and their work can save lives.

> If they understand how volcanoes behave, geologists can better predict when one will be dangerous and warn people to evacuate the area.

Some volcanologists study volcanoes that are no longer active by looking at deposits from past eruptions to try to understand clues from the past. We can better predict the future if we understand how volcanoes changed the earth in the past.[10]

KEY QUESTIONS

- Why do volcanoes form?
- How can volcanoes change the landscape?
- What benefits do we get from volcanoes?
- How and why do scientists study volcanoes?

ROCK SOLID

Few colleges teach volcanology. Most people study geology if they want to go into this field.

Text-to-World Connection

● ● ● ● ● ● ● ●

Research which active volcano is closest to you. What type of volcano is it? How is it being monitored? What is the volcano doing right now?

MAGMA ROCK DEMONSTRATION

Magma can break through the earth's surface in several ways. Its behavior is not always predictable. Model what might happen when magma slowly pushes to the earth's surface.

- **Use scissors to puncture the bottom of an empty, clean yogurt container (single-serving size).** Twist the scissors to make the hole the size of a toothpaste tube opening.

- **Push a toothpaste tube opening through the hole so the full tube of toothpaste hangs below.**

- **Add dirt to fill the container about two-thirds of the way to the top.** The loose dirt represents the ground surface. The toothpaste represents magma rock.

- **Squeeze the toothpaste.** What happens? How does it change if you squeeze the toothpaste slowly or quickly?

- **What can you learn about the behavior of magma from this experiment?** How does oozing magma differ from a volcano that erupts explosively?

> **To investigate more,** visit Oregon State University's Volcano World. You'll find virtual field trips, photos, volcano games, and much more.
>
> 🔍 Oregon State volcano

Chapter 3 ▶
Earthquakes Shake Us Up

Why do earthquakes happen?

Earthquakes are a result of tectonic plates moving in certain ways under the crust of the earth.

A sudden grinding sound fills the air. The floor moves under your feet like a ship bobbing up and down on waves. Everything starts to shake and rattle. Water sloshes out of a glass. The vibrating table sends the glass skittering toward the edge. It falls and shatters on the floor.

In a minute or two, it's over. Did a semi-truck ram your house? Did a giant stomp past?

No, it was an earthquake! Did you remember the instructions for what to do in an earthquake? You were supposed to "duck, cover, and hold on" to stay safe from falling objects. But it all happened so fast!

Family and friends call or message to say they're safe. Aftershocks hit throughout the day, but they are smaller vibrations as the ground finishes settling. Still, every time the ground shakes, you tense and wait to see if it will get worse. The news plays constant coverage. Experts explain the science behind what happened, in between shots of cracked walls and grocery stores with food that fell off the shelves.

WHO'S AT FAULT?

Large earthquakes can devastate the landscape and cause major damage to buildings. They can seriously injure people—and cause thousands of deaths. Yet, most earthquakes are so small, people never even notice them. In fact, hundreds of earthquakes happen every day! It takes delicate scientific equipment to record these small quakes.

Every year, about 50,000 earthquakes are large enough for people to notice. About 100 are serious enough to cause major damage, if they happen close to cities. On average, once a year, a huge earthquake causes many deaths and enormous property damage. Yet, depending on where you live, chances are good that you've never felt an earthquake.

Earthquake damage in Italy

FORE AND AFTER

An earthquake sequence may start with foreshocks, which are smaller earthquakes before the biggest shock. These can only be identified as foreshocks after the largest earthquake comes. More small quakes called aftershocks may follow the largest shock. Thousands of aftershocks may follow an earthquake during the course of weeks, months, or even years. Two large earthquakes struck Christchurch, New Zealand, in 2010 and 2011. They were followed by smaller aftershocks for at least seven years. Foreshocks and aftershocks can be quite large and cause damage.

During an earthquake, move away from hazardous areas. Then, "drop, cover, and hold on!" Learn more from the U.S. Department of Homeland Security.

 ready gov earthquakes

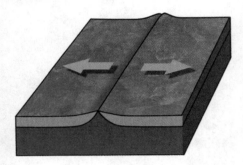

divergent boundary

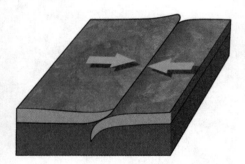

convergent boundary

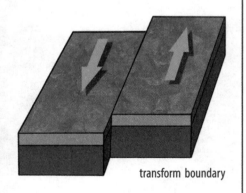

transform boundary

Remember how the earth's plates move against each other? You probably won't be surprised to hear that plate movement causes most earthquakes. Big earthquakes are most common at geologic fault lines. In a fault, pieces of the earth's crust press against each other, trying to go in different directions and causing pressure to build up.

Sometimes, the plates slip suddenly, releasing energy all at once. This released energy causes vibrations called seismic waves. And seismic waves cause the sudden shaking of the ground—an earthquake!

Most seismic activity happens at three types of plate boundaries. At divergent boundaries, two plates move away from each other. This allows molten rock from the mantle to erupt along the opening and form new crust. The Red Sea and the Great Rift Valley in Africa were formed this way. Earthquakes along these spreading zones are usually fairly small. At convergent boundaries, the plates collide rather than separate.

If this happens on land, the edges of the plates crumple and are pushed up. This can form huge, high mountain ranges, such as the Himalayas.

Plates can also collide where a continental plate meets an oceanic plate. In that case, the thinner and more flexible oceanic plate sinks beneath the thicker and more rigid continental plate. This process, called subduction, forms deep ocean trenches and may also form a line of volcanoes. About 80 percent of earthquakes happen at convergent boundaries, where plates collide.

The third type of plate boundary is a transform or lateral fault, where two tectonic plates slide past each other. The San Andreas Fault, which makes California prone to earthquakes, is an example of lateral plate motion.

Scientists can now map the major fault lines between tectonic plates. As you might expect, earthquakes are more common in these places. Most of the world's earthquakes take place in the Ring of Fire, where several tectonic plates meet.

The Ring of Fire runs along coastal areas where many people live, including the western coasts of North and South America, Alaska, Japan, New Zealand, and New Guinea.

The Ring of Fire

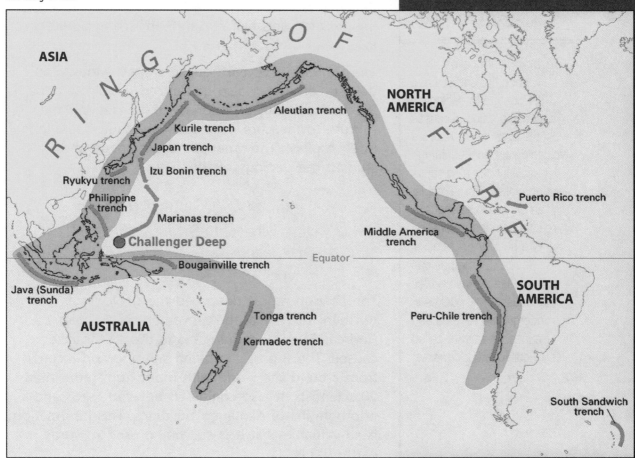

Watch a video about the San Andreas Fault from the Discovery Channel.

 Discovery San Andreas Fault

AND THEN THERE'S . . .

Tectonic earthquakes occur when the earth's crust breaks due to geological forces. If a volcano causes the earth to move, it's a volcanic earthquake. Human activity can also cause earthquakes. For example, an explosion earthquake results from the detonation of a nuclear or chemical device. Explosions can also release seismic waves that cause small quakes in underground caverns and mines. These are called collapse earthquakes.

LEARNING FROM DISASTER

In California, two plates slide against each other at a transform, or lateral, fault called the San Andreas Fault, causing frequent earthquakes. In 1906, a deadly earthquake nearly wiped out San Francisco. At 5:12 a.m. on April 18, people awoke to violent shaking and sharp shock waves. Machines recorded the waves as far as Germany, 5,650 miles away. The ground split apart in a crack 296 miles long, with a 20-foot-wide surface gap in places. That gap was sometimes even larger underground.

The earthquake caused damage that started a fire. Between the earthquake and fire, more than 3,000 people died and half of San Francisco's population lost their homes.

The San Francisco earthquake caused widespread devastation, but it also galvanized people to act. Researchers walked hundreds of miles along the rupture to measure how much the fault had slipped in each place. They mapped the damage and studied the geology of the area.

Later, in 1908, all the scientific work was compiled in a document called the Lawson report.

The Lawson report described the geology of northern California, the movement of the San Andreas Fault, and the damage the earthquake caused. The report combined seismograph records from around the world with input from more than 20 scientists. It also contained detailed maps and photographs of damaged buildings. This information is so valuable that it is still being used to study earthquakes.

The report revealed that the design and construction of buildings affected how they were damaged. The local geology, especially the type of soil or rock under a building, also played a role. For example, structures built on solid rock had the least amount of damage. Soft, sedimentary soils experienced some of the strongest shaking. On marshy ground or areas that had been artificially filled, structures were greatly damaged.

In some areas, the ground even seemed to liquefy! Loose sand and silt that is soaked with water can behave like a liquid during an earthquake, in a process known as liquefaction. The wet soil might flow down slopes or erupt from the ground as if the sand was boiling. On this unstable ground, buildings can shake mightily and even collapse. Buried water and sewer pipes may twist and break. Surviving buildings might be tipped at an angle.

The Lawson report led to the development of new theories about earthquake behavior. Before 1906, people thought that earthquakes caused faults instead of the other way around. Because of the research that went into the report, scientists discovered that as tectonic plates move, pressure builds up along the fault lines. The ground may suddenly slip, releasing years of strain, generating seismic waves that travel underground and produce shaking.

The 1908 Lawson report showed that communities built on soft ground experienced the most damage from the earthquake. Yet, people rebuilt in these same parts of San Francisco. They even used earthquake debris as landfill. These areas sustained heavy damage once again during the 1989 Loma Prieta earthquake. Why do you think people made the same mistakes even after they knew more about the science behind earthquakes?[11]

You can see the damage from the 1906 earthquake in this rare footage of the aftermath.

 Cal historical society earthquake

ROCK SOLID

Scientists have created detailed pictures of seismic activity within the San Andreas Fault system. Maps now predict where shaking is likely to be the strongest. These maps help city planners make decisions about where to build homes, schools, and hospitals.

SEISMIC WAVES

Today, machines called seismographs, or seismometers, measure seismic waves at more than 1,000 sites in California. These machines record the duration and intensity of any shaking and provide data for scientists to analyze.

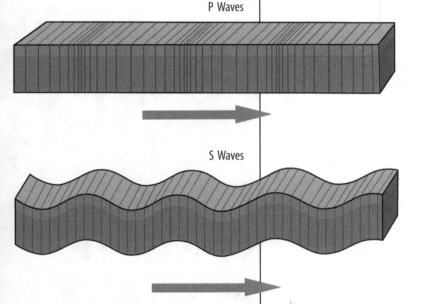

P Waves

S Waves

What exactly are they measuring? Earthquakes produce three different types of waves, which travel at different speeds. The fastest are called primary waves, or P waves. They can pass through solids, liquids, and gases. As they pass through the earth, materials are slightly pushed together and pulled apart.

Secondary waves, or S waves, start at the same time as primary waves, but they travel at about half the speed. They can travel only through solids, not liquids and gases. They shake material up and down or side to side.

Meanwhile, surface waves move along the earth's surface, not through its interior. They cause the ground to shake from side to side or roll up and down. They are the slowest waves, but they cause the largest ground movements and, therefore, the most damage on the surface.

Seismometers measure when each type of wave hits each location, so that scientists can calculate the speed of the waves. By studying the behavior of seismic waves, scientists can infer what is happening inside the earth.

This helped them figure out that the inner core of the earth is solid and the outer core is molten—seismic waves behave differently in each area.[12]

MARKING MAGNITUDE

Scientists describe the size of an earthquake by its magnitude. A larger number means a bigger earthquake. You probably won't notice an earthquake with a magnitude of less than 3.0—you might feel a slight shaking and think a large truck is driving by. The energy released by a magnitude 3.0 earthquake is comparable to a large lightning bolt. A sensitive machine could detect it. Hundreds of these small earthquakes happen every day.

The scale is not a straight line. For each step up in magnitude, an earthquake releases 30 times more energy. At magnitude 4.0, people are likely to notice the earthquake—items on shelves shake and rattle and might even fall and break. But a magnitude 4.0 quake shouldn't do any major damage.

By magnitude 5.0, an earthquake has energy comparable to an average tornado. You'll definitely feel it! And if the earthquake occurs close enough to buildings and structures, they will likely be damaged. A magnitude 6.0 earthquake is considered "strong." Property damage may extend for 100 miles from the quake's point of origin. An earthquake with a magnitude of 6.0 to 6.9 can destroy a large city if the structures are not built to withstand shaking.

A magnitude 7.0 earthquake is "major" and causes serious damage to large areas. Expect to see billions of dollars in damage and some loss of life.

MAGNITUDE 9.2

The largest earthquake in the United States, as of this writing, hit Alaska in 1964. It was the second largest earthquake ever recorded. It had a magnitude of 9.2 and lasted about 4½ minutes. Fortunately, the region was not highly populated. Still, 15 people died from the initial earthquake and another 116 died in the tsunamis and landslides that followed.

Scientists used to use a mathematical formula called the Richter scale to measure earthquakes, but today, we simply refer to the magnitude of an earthquake, because many different scales are used to arrive at these numbers.

● ● ● ● ● ● ● ● ●

The 2010 earthquake in Haiti was a magnitude 7.0 earthquake.

Major earthquakes happen more than once per month.

An earthquake of magnitude 8.0 to 8.9 is called "great." Serious damage can affect an area hundreds of miles across. The deadliest known quake hit China in 1556 CE, killing an estimated 830,000 people. Scientists think it was probably between 8.0 and 8.3 in magnitude. The death toll was so high because it hit a highly populated area with many stone buildings that toppled. Great earthquakes happen once every year, on average.

At 9.0 to 9.9, the damage is likely to be devastating for several thousand miles. The 1964 Alaska earthquake was in this range, which is still considered "great."

The largest earthquake ever recorded was the 1960 Valdivia earthquake in Chile. It measured 9.5 in magnitude and created a tsunami. Together, the earthquake and tsunami killed an estimated 5,700 people. An "epic" earthquake of magnitude 10.0 or higher has never been recorded.

INTENSE!

Magnitude describes how much seismic energy an earthquake releases. But that's not the whole picture. People experience an earthquake differently depending on how close they are to its center.

Let's look at an example. On January 17, 1994, an earthquake hit Northridge, California, with a magnitude of 6.9. That's a "strong" earthquake, and very close to a "major" one. It also hit a highly populated area. You might expect a high death toll, yet only 51 people died. Why didn't the Northridge quake do more damage?

The magnitude of an earthquake is measured where the quake originates. An earthquake that is deep underground or far from cities can be powerful in magnitude but not do much damage. Intensity is a better way to measure an earthquake's ability to do damage. Intensity is the way an earthquake affects a specific place. The intensity lessens as you get farther away from the source. Intensity is also affected by how deep the center of the earthquake is.

A map showing the different intensities of the 1968 earthquake in Illinois

DEADLY WAVES

A fault slipping under the ocean may cause the ocean floor to suddenly thrust upward. This pushes the water above that area upward as well. As that water sinks back into the ocean, it sets off waves. By the time the waves reach shore, they come in like fast tides, quickly surging up the land. The fast currents sweep away anything in their path—this debris can cause further damage as it hits things.

Seismic waves travel about 100 times faster than tsunami waves. Depending on how far the earthquake was from shore, a tsunami may follow minutes or hours later. That can give scientists time to predict a tsunami and warn people to evacuate.

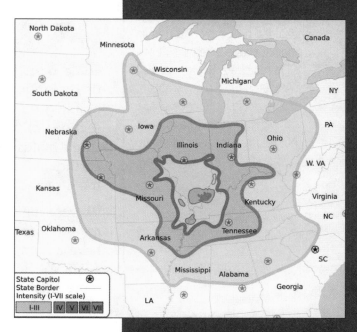

If the center is near the surface, the earthquake will feel more intense than if the center is deep underground. The local geography also plays a part, since solid rock will not shake as much as soft ground.

> Fortunately for the people of Northridge, the intensity of the 1994 quake wasn't as high as its magnitude.[13]

UNDER STRESS

In geology, stress is a force that acts on rocks. Areas of rock can be stressed if they have weight pressing down from above, if they are squeezed from the sides, if they are pulled apart under tension, or if they have forces moving in opposite directions. How a rock responds to stress depends on the rock type, the surrounding temperature, the amount of pressure, and other factors. A rock may respond by fracturing, or breaking. But, in some cases, the rock may return to its original shape when the stress is removed. Rock may also undergo plastic deformation, meaning it changes shape without breaking and does not return to its original shape when the stress is removed.

PREDICTING FUTURE EARTHQUAKES

Seismologists can identify areas likely to have earthquakes. One of the areas expected to have another large one is San Francisco. But when?

Right now, scientists can only calculate the potential for future earthquakes. For example, will a major earthquake hit California in the next 30 years? Scientists say there is a 60-percent chance that the answer is yes for Southern California. The probability is 67 percent for the San Francisco Bay Area.

Some parts of the San Andreas Fault have frequent tiny earthquakes, which seem to keep stress from building up along the fault line. But, in other areas, sections of the fault are locked together. The seismic strain builds up without the release provided by tiny earthquakes. It might take a major quake to release the stresses in these sections.

It's very difficult to know when that major quake might happen. Part of the reason is because we don't have a complete record of seismic activity before 1850. We do know that between 1850 and 1906, more than a dozen major earthquakes hit the area.

Then, the next 70 years saw only one earthquake of a similar size. Northern California was fairly quiet, seismically speaking. After a period of heavy seismic activity, a quiet period may follow as the stress builds up again.

However, the region may be returning to a period of greater seismic activity. Scientists believe earthquakes as large as the 1906 San Francisco quake happen about every 200 years. Smaller, but still major, earthquakes happen more often. According to some geologists, a major quake is likely before 2032.

Seismologists dream of being able to accurately predict earthquakes, but for now, they have only small signs to work with. Before an earthquake, the speed and frequency of seismic waves may change. Groundwater might slightly change in level. The amount of magnetism in rocks could also change.

> Much more study is needed to predict when an earthquake will happen, but even a few seconds of warning can save lives.[14]

PREVENTING EARTHQUAKES

Is it possible to not only predict, but prevent future earthquakes? Human activity can actually cause small earthquakes. For example, earthquakes can happen in mines that go very deep or when nuclear bombs are tested underground. Certainly, we could make progress by changing our own behavior.

Some human influence can be a positive in seismic terms. Remember, small earthquakes can release major strain and help prevent large earthquakes.

ROCK SOLID

Paleoseismology is the study of ancient earthquakes. Specialists in this field examine how rock or soil layers were disrupted by prehistoric earthquakes. This helps predict future fault behavior.

Learn about earthquakes in a video from National Geographic.

 National Geographic Earthquakes 101

SEISMOLOGISTS AT WORK

Seismologists are scientists who study the movement of waves through the earth, such as those that cause earthquakes. These scientists might work in the field, surveying sites and collecting samples to later be tested in a lab. They travel to areas that have suffered a recent earthquake to study its effects. Seismologists also study tsunamis and landslides caused by earthquakes. Some monitor active volcanoes for seismic activity. They might write reports and make maps. A seismologist may work for a university, a research center, a government group, or a private company. Not all seismologists focus on earthquakes. Many work for oil and gas companies studying seismic waves caused by explosions, construction equipment, and even large trucks. This can help them discover underground sources of oil and natural gas.

Some oil drilling involves injecting fluids into deep wells in a process known as hydraulic fracturing, or fracking. This breaks up the underground rock. Artificially shaking the ground this way can also release some of the seismic strain. It might be possible to inject fluids into fault zones in order to release energy. Causing a small, controlled earthquake might prevent a larger, more serious quake later.

But would you want to be responsible for starting an earthquake? What if it grows larger than expected and does major damage?

Humans must address the practical, legal, and ethical questions before pursuing this option.

It may be a more realistic option to try to prevent earthquakes from doing much damage. Understanding how the ground moves during an earthquake helps engineers design buildings to resist shaking. In an earthquake, most damage and death comes from buildings and bridges collapsing. Making structures that withstand intense ground motion can save lives. Geologists can help determine which sites are best for different types of buildings and can recommend the right materials to use.

States and countries where earthquakes are common often have laws requiring buildings to be made in a way that withstands earthquakes. Skyscrapers may float on systems of ball bearings, springs, and padded cylinders, which act as shock absorbers. The buildings don't sit directly on the ground, so when an earthquake hits, they sway a few feet but should not crumble.

Another technique puts a large, very heavy mass at the top of the building. When seismic waves hit, the large mass sways in the opposite direction from the rest of the building. This can reduce the overall sway of the building up to 40 percent.

> Unfortunately, not every country has strict building laws to prevent earthquake damage.

In 2010, an earthquake measuring 7.0 magnitude killed more than 200,000 people in Haiti. Many of the buildings there were poorly constructed.

More industrialized countries often have stricter building codes, but, sometimes, older buildings are still not up to current codes. In addition, building codes have usually been designed to protect people but not buildings. In the Christchurch, New Zealand, earthquake, few people died, but the entire downtown had to be closed because damaged buildings made the whole area dangerous. It took years to rebuild. California is considering new building regulations that would keep new buildings usable after a major earthquake. Then, people could return to their homes and jobs within a few weeks, instead of years.

KEY QUESTIONS

- **Should the goals of the scientific community focus more on preventing earthquakes or predicting earthquakes?**
- **What are some of the ethical issues about releasing seismic strain through artificial processes?**

Hear a seismologist give a short introduction to earthquake monitoring work by the British Geological Survey.

 BGS seismology

VOCAB LAB

Write down what you think each word means. What root words can you find to help you? What does the context of the word tell you?

aftershock, convergent boundary, divergent boundary, intensity, liquefaction, magnitude, seismic wave, seismologist, and **transform boundary**.

Compare your definitions with those of your friends or classmates. Did you all come up with the same meanings? Turn to the text and glossary if you need help.

EARTHQUAKE IN A BOX

Scientists use models to better understand complex concepts and processes. Model what happens during an earthquake and see what new things you discover.

- **Using building materials such as wooden blocks, heavy paper, thin paper, and interlocking plastic blocks such as Lego bricks, build some structures inside a shallow box or box lid.** Fold sheets of paper and balance pieces of building material on each other. Do not attach the building pieces together with tape or glue.

- **Gently shake the box.** What happens? If some structures are still standing, shake a little bit harder. What happens now?

- **Now, rebuild your structures.** This time try different ways of attaching the pieces.

- **Gently shake the box again.** What happens?

- **Put a layer of sand or gravel in the bottom of the box.** How does this new "ground" affect the structures when you shake the box?

- **What can you learn about how different building materials and different land surfaces affect buildings in an earthquake?** Did heavy, solid pieces survive better? Or did lighter, flexible pieces do better?

Text-to-World Connection

● ● ● ● ● ● ● ●

Do you live in an area prone to earthquakes? What safety measures do you have in place?

> **To investigate more,** research what building materials are recommended for areas prone to earthquakes. What are the advantages and disadvantages of different building materials?

Chapter 4 ▷
Erosion: The Power of Water and Air

LOTS OF ELEMENTS COME TOGETHER TO MAKE UP ROCKS AND MINERALS!

Why is the relationship between water, air, and the earth important?

BUT AREN'T ROCKS JUST MADE OF . . . ROCK? AND DIRT?

MORE OR LESS, BUT WITHOUT WATER, THEY COULD NEVER COME TOGETHER!

WATER AND WIND BOTH PLAY HUGE PARTS IN FORMING ROCKS AND STONE!

Water and air have unique effects on the makeup of the earth, and can cause a lot of change in both a short time and a very, very long time!

● ● ● ● ● ● ● ●

Australia is home to Uluru, also known as Ayers Rock. This reddish-orange rock formation rises 1,142 feet above the flat surrounding plain. Walking around its base takes about three and half hours. Every year, up to half a million people flock to see this majestic sight that holds cultural and spiritual significance for the local indigenous tribes.

But how did this massive rock get there? Uluru did not form from explosive volcanic forces or even thrusting tectonic plates. This majestic landmark exists because of weathering and erosion.

Weathering is the wearing down of materials from the crust of the earth. Erosion moves those materials away. Wind, precipitation, and ice can all cause weathering and erosion. While tectonic plate movement and volcanoes can cause large, sudden changes to the landscape, quieter forces can also create drastic changes to the earth. In the long run, weathering and erosion can have the most dramatic effect of all, as we can see with Uluru.

The story of Uluru is a long and complex one that began around 500 million years ago. High mountains composed mainly of granite eroded, and those sediments collected and hardened into sandstone. As time passed, an inland sea deposited limestone, sand, and mud around that rock. The weight of these deposits compressed the original sandstone into a hard mass. Then, the softer, surrounding sediments began to wear away.

Uluru emerged with the passing of hundreds of millions of years—not because it grew higher, but because the surrounding land dropped lower. In fact, more than 8,000 feet of Uluru is still buried underground.

Let's take a closer look at weathering, erosion, and the soil that's affected by these geological forces!

Uluru is a reddish-orange color because air oxidizes the iron in the surface rock.

LIVING SOILS

Not all sediment hardens into rocks. Some becomes part of soil. Soil is made up of minerals, organic matter, living organisms, gas, and water. Depending on the size of the minerals, soil may be considered silt, clay, or sand. Soil organic matter is decomposing plants and animals. Soil also contains living things, which may include mammals, birds, insects, and microbes. Soils absorb and release gases and water. Plants grow in soil because they have water and nutrients from the decaying organic matter. Without soil for growing our food, we couldn't survive!

TAKE IT AWAY

Weathering breaks down solid rock into smaller pieces called sediment. Several forces can break rocks into smaller pieces. Ice wedging starts when water seeps into cracks in the rock and then freezes. Water expands as it turns from a liquid to a solid, which wedges apart the rock. As the water repeatedly freezes and thaws, expanding and shrinking, it breaks the rocks into pieces.

A similar process works without water. Thermal weathering is caused by a great difference in temperature between day and night. Rocks expand in the daytime heat and then quickly contract as night falls. After days of this cycle, the rocks might break apart.

Plants can split rocks by growing in cracks and wedging them open.

Abrasion happens when one rock bumps against another, such as when rocks fall down a cliff. Another form of abrasion weathering happens when glaciers move, and rocks embedded in the bottom of the ice scrape against the rocks below. Flowing water and strong winds can also cause abrasion, as can windblown sand moving across deserts. Abrasion smooths rocks and rounds their edges. Have you ever seen beach glass? The smooth edges and rounded shape is caused by abrasion.

These forms of mechanical weathering do not change the rock itself. The smaller pieces have the same composition as the original larger one—every piece has the same minerals in the same proportions.

ROCK SOLID

The moon has no atmosphere, which means no wind or rain and no weathering. That's why the footprints left by astronauts in 1969 remain!

Chemical weathering, on the other hand, is the result of a chemical reaction that changes the minerals in the rock, altering the rock's composition. Have you heard of acid rain? This occurs when pollutants in the air combine with falling rain, making the rain more acidic than typical rainwater. The resulting acid rain can damage the surfaces of buildings and monuments.

Even unpolluted air and water can cause chemical weathering. For example, iron rusts when exposed to the air, in a process called oxidation. Also, some minerals, including salt, can be dissolved by water. When water dissolves some parts of a rock and washes them away, the process is called leaching. These are both examples of chemical weathering.

Learn all about soils from Scitable by Nature Education.

 Scitable Soils

These boulders in Australia show both chemical and mechanical weathering.

ROCK SOLID

Can you spot these forces at work in your own neighborhood? When sidewalks crumble or rain washes mud into the street, that's weathering and erosion.

Both mechanical and chemical weathering are often followed by erosion. Weathering breaks rocks into sediment, while erosion moves the sediment to new places. For example, water washes sediment, or even large rocks, downhill. Wind moves sand, dust, and tiny pieces of rock through the air. Glaciers carve new scenery as they scrape across the landscape, carrying sediment of all sizes.

Gravity can carry both large pieces of rock and small sediment downhill. This can happen quickly, as in a landslide, or so slowly that it takes years to see the difference.

As millions of years pass, weathering and erosion can wear down mountains into hills or flat plains.

Erosion and weathering can also create canyons, which are deep, narrow valleys with steep sides. Canyons are often formed by rivers, which cut through the rock during thousands or millions of years. The canyon may still contain a river today, or the river may have dried up or moved elsewhere. Glaciers can also cut through land to create canyons.

Geologists love canyons because the steep cliffs show layers of rock that can tell the history of the area going back millions of years. They can see how the climate changed, as the thickness of different layers and the patterns of erosion show wet and dry periods. Fossils show what organisms were alive at different times. Paleontologists can estimate the age of the fossils by the layer in which they are found.

Erosion caused by agricultural use in the United States

In wet regions, rocks undergo more chemical breakdown, but plants sometimes bind the soil and prevent erosion. Dry climates such as deserts see less chemical breakdown, but rocks are more exposed to mechanical breakdown through ice wedging, thermal weathering, and abrasion. If heavy rain does fall, it may cause landslides and flash floods that carry huge amounts of debris.

BUILDING PLATEAUS

The four major landforms on Earth are mountains, plains, hills, and plateaus. A plateau is a relatively flat, elevated landform that rises sharply above the surrounding area. A plateau can form when tectonic plates slowly collide and lift up a section of land, as with the Colorado Plateau. It has been rising for more than 10 million years at a rate of about 0.01 inches a year. Volcanic forces can also form plateaus, when many small volcanic eruptions release lava flows that slowly build up the land over time, as with the Columbia Plateau in the Pacific Northwest. Erosion often influences the shape of a plateau as wind, rain, and rivers erode away soft rock. The remaining plateau may be capped by a hard, durable surface called caprock. Erosion may wear down a large plateau into similar flat-topped features called mesas and buttes. A mesa is smaller than a plateau, and a butte is even smaller than a mesa, although definitions for the specific sizes vary. Eventually, erosion may sculpt much smaller, more peculiar landforms, such as arches and hoodoos.

Learn more about plateaus in this video.

 Plateau Mesa and Butte

The Grand Canyon creates its own weather! The sudden changes in elevation affect temperature and precipitation in the canyon.

Some Native American nations made apartment-style shelters called cliff dwellings on canyon ledges. Living high on the cliffs offers protection from the hot sun and hostile neighbors. The Hopi and Navajo often used box canyons—canyons open on one end—as natural corrals for sheep and cattle. They simply built a gate on the open end to keep the animals inside. People and animals have also used caves within canyons for shelter.

● ● ● ● ● ● ● ●

When the earth's processes work together, they can create remarkable formations. For example, Utah in the United States is known for incredible canyons and unusual rock formations. Bryce Canyon, in southwestern Utah, was part of a huge lake and floodplain around 50 million years ago. Streams eroded particles of rock into the lower basin. These sediments cemented together in sedimentary rocks, including sandstone, limestone, and mudstone. Later, plate tectonics forced one plate beneath another, thrusting some of the land higher.

In the last few million years, the descending plate began to break apart, allowing heat to rise. This heat elevated the Four Corners area of the Colorado Plateau. Finally, weathering and erosion, primarily through ice and rain, broke apart the rocks. The different types of rock are more or less sensitive to acidic water. As some dissolved, they left strange and beautiful formations behind: arches, windows, and tall, thin spires of rock called hoodoos. Wind polishes and shapes these features.[15]

Hoodoos in Bryce Canyon, Utah

A natural arch in Bryce Canyon, Utah

ROCK SOLID

Some rocks in the Grand Canyon are 1.8 billion years old, while the youngest rock layer is 270 million years old. However, the canyon itself is much younger. It's hard to state a precise age, since the canyon formed during billions of years and gets deeper every year.

THE POWER OF WATER

Water can cause noticeable erosion quickly, as when a flood carries boulders down a streambed or washes away a road. The effects of water are even more powerful as hundreds, thousands, or millions of years pass. Water can form gullies, reroute rivers, change coastlines, and cut deep canyons into the land.

A canyon forms when erosion creates a valley with sides that are nearly vertical, in a process called downcutting. The Grand Canyon in Arizona cuts through the ground for 277 miles. That's longer than the state of California is wide! The canyon slices into the ground with walls as steep as stairs in places, while plunging an average of 1 mile deep. That's more than four times the height of the Empire State Building. The rocks that make up the canyon walls are older than the dinosaurs.

What formed this incredible landmark? Water!

A MISSING LINK

An unconformity in rocks means no rocks were preserved from a certain time. Either no rocks were formed then or they all eroded away. Small unconformities are common. The Great Unconformity, however, is a gap of 250 to 1,200 million years. The rocks in the Grand Canyon clearly show this gap. What happened to the rocks from those millions of years? *National Geographic* shares one theory in this article.

🔍 Nat Geo missing glaciers

The Grand Canyon in Arizona

ROCK SOLID

When precipitation falls as snow, it can stay on the surface of the ground for days or even months. Once temperatures rise, the snow melts and behaves like rain.

At the bottom of the Grand Canyon, you'll find the Colorado River. This river averages about 300 feet in width—not especially wide. It flows through the canyon at an average speed of about 4 miles per hour—not particularly fast. So how did the river cut this enormous gash?

Well, it's been working at it for 5 to 6 million years.

The area's history actually starts much earlier. About 2 billion years ago, igneous and metamorphic rocks formed here. Then, many layers of sedimentary rocks piled on top. Plate tectonics thrust a rock layer from sea level up to an elevation of 9,000 feet—to form the Colorado Plateau.

The Grand Canyon was formed when the Colorado River cut down into the earth, eroding away rocks. During floods, the river carried away even large boulders. As millions of years passed, the Colorado River cut into the plateau, a few inches every year. Now, the famous Grand Canyon is an example of how powerful the forces of weathering can be.

WHEN THE RAIN COMES DOWN

As we've seen, rivers are surprisingly powerful. Fast-flowing water can move even large boulders. But what about rain? Rain is sporadic and can be quite light. It might seem as though rain only serves to make the ground soggy for a short time.

But rain can be a force of nature strong enough to change the landscape.

How water behaves on the land depends on where it falls and what the ground is like. Sandy soil soaks up rain more easily than dense clay soil. Roads, sidewalks, and parking lots don't soak up water because they're coated in asphalt, so the water runs off. Streets are designed to funnel the water elsewhere, typically into creeks and streams, but it's risky to funnel extra water into these natural features. Some channels can't handle the extra water so quickly, and the extra volume of water can lead to flooding.

Water flow is also affected by topography, both the natural and human-made features of an area. Water runs off mountains and hills into valleys and canyons. On uneven land, water drains downhill and keeps going until it joins a stream, finds a low spot to settle, or soaks into the ground.

It's important to know how water behaves so people can direct it in appropriate ways. They can drain rainfall away from structures and off streets in ways that won't overwhelm natural channels. Vegetation slows water runoff, so people can grow certain plants or trees on slopes to help with erosion. These techniques work most of the time. But, sometimes, rain falls so heavily it creates a natural disaster.

TECH TALK

Technology helps geologists make accurate maps. Lidar (Light Detection and Ranging) uses light from a laser to measure distances. Airplanes or helicopters can carry lidar instruments to take measurements from the air. Lidar can detect how high the land is with an accuracy of about 6 inches and can map the land surface and show subtle elevation changes. These detailed maps can predict areas at risk of flooding so city planners can design communities that avoid and prevent damage. Lidar is also used to assess other types of hazards, including lava flows, landslides, and tsunamis.

BURIED IN WATER

Flooding is a natural hazard related to geology. Floods can happen when rain falls for several days or when heavy rain falls quickly in what's known as a flash flood. Floods can also result from damage to a water control structure, such as a dam, or from debris or ice clogging a river channel and causing the river to overflow. About 75 percent of all presidential disaster declarations in the United States involve flooding. Have you experienced a flood?

Floods are dangerous because water can rise and move quickly. Even just 6 inches of fast-moving floodwater can knock over a person. Twelve inches can carry away a small car. Yet people see shallow water and think it's safe to cross. More than half of all flood-related drownings happen when someone drives a vehicle into floodwater. People who walk into floodwaters make up the next largest category of drownings. In the United States, dozens of people die in floods every year. Worldwide, the numbers can reach into the thousands.

Flooding after a hurricane in South Carolina, 2015

credit: Petty Officer 1st Class Stephen Lehmann

Millions of people are affected by flooding in different ways every year.

They might lose their homes and belongings, crops, and livestock. Businesses can be destroyed, putting people out of work. Power can go out for weeks, leaving people without electricity. If city water systems are damaged, people may not have clean water to drink, and without working waste disposal systems, sewage backs up and can spread disease.

While floods can be devastating for human populations, they can also have a positive effect on the environment. They refill aquifers and wetlands while moving soil and nutrients throughout the landscape. Flooding is a necessary part of the life cycle of many aquatic animals, as they trigger migration and breeding. To some extent, floods are a healthy part of nature. However, people have changed the landscape in ways that change flood patterns, and flood damage tends to be worse where people have made the greatest changes.

Geologists try to help communities understand the risks of flooding so they can avoid the dangers. Floodplain studies reveal what might happen to rivers after heavy rains. Geological maps can also show areas most at risk. They describe the land elevation and soil and rock types, which show where water will be soaked in and where it will run off.

Geology is the study of the earth, and water is an important part of our planet. Geologists have to understand the effects of water on the landscape and on human structures. That way, they can help communities survive water disasters, show people how to use water in sustainable ways, and predict where erosion and other shifts in the landscape are going to happen and prepare for them.[16]

VOCAB LAB

Write down what you think each word means. What root words can you find to help you? What does the context of the word tell you?

abrasion, **chemical weathering**, **glacier**, **leaching**, **natural disaster**, **runoff**, **thermal weathering**, and **topography**.

Compare your definitions with those of your friends or classmates. Did you all come up with the same meanings? Turn to the text and glossary if you need help.

KEY QUESTIONS

- **What is erosion? How is it different from weathering?**

- **What causes floods? Why are they dangerous?**

- **How can geologists help communities prepare for or prevent flooding?**

EROSION EXPERIMENT

Forces such as rain, wind, and glacial ice can cause erosion. What effects can these different forces have?

- **Take three plastic containers, about shoebox size.** Fill each halfway with soil. Pile the soil toward one end of each container to make a sloping hill.

- **Simulate wind erosion in one container.** Blow air through a straw onto the top of the hill. What happens? Blow air from a fan across the soil. Start on the lowest setting and increase it. What changes when the wind gets stronger?

- **Simulate water erosion in the next container.** Use a spray bottle to spray the top of the soil. What happens? Next, spray the dirt with a hose. How do the effects change with more water or water poured more rapidly?

- **Simulate glacial erosion using ice cubes.** Place ice cubes at the top of the hill. What happens when you nudge them downhill? Which of these means of erosion has the greatest effect? Under what circumstances?

- **Try these experiments on flat soil.** Is the soil still changed in the same way? What happens if you add groundcover, such as scattering wood chips, grass, pine needles, or rocks on the soil?

> **To investigate more,** look for signs of erosion in your neighborhood. Watch for hazards such as unstable ground or poison ivy. Can you tell if the erosion was caused by wind, water, or ice? How did human activity contribute to it?

Chapter 5 ▷
Surface Water and Groundwater

WATER HAS A HUGE IMPACT ON THE FORMATION OF ROCKS AND MINERALS!

Why do geologists study water?

Humans can't live without water, and keeping the waterways safe and unpolluted is an important part of keeping the planet healthy. Geologists play a major role in this!

● ● ● ● ● ● ● ● ●

When you look at a picture of Earth taken from space, what's the first thing you notice? Maybe how blue it is? All that blue is evidence that our planet is a very watery place. Lucky for us! Water was key to the development of life on our planet. Without it, we wouldn't be here, and neither would any of the mammals, birds, reptiles, amphibians, or bacteria that make our world the biodiverse haven it is.

It's a good thing oceans cover about 74 percent of the earth's surface, right? The only problem is, we really need fresh water, not salty seawater.

We need clean, fresh water to drink. We also need it for cooking food, bathing, washing clothes and dishes, watering gardens, and other daily tasks. On a larger scale, agriculture depends on fresh water for irrigation, and most manufacturing processes use water as well. Lakes and rivers provide fresh water, but these don't exist everywhere that people live. Rain tends to be seasonal in most places, meaning it doesn't fall all year round.

Surface water can easily be polluted. Garbage, sewage, and chemicals should not be dumped into rivers, lakes, or water drains—yet, sometimes, they are. And storms can cause chemicals from cities and farmland to flow into lakes or rivers, while erosion can result in sediment in water sources.

All of this means that surface water can easily be contaminated with bacteria and other harmful substances.

When that surface water becomes drinking water, it can cause illnesses, such as diarrhea, typhoid, cholera, dysentery, and hepatitis. These diseases can be deadly, especially for young children.

Digging deep wells can limit some of this pollution, but governments still spend billions of dollars trying to control pollution and protect surface water, and, therefore, our water supplies. Hydrology is the branch of geology focused on the study of water, and hydrologists are the scientists who study water.

An aerial view of a polluted body of water in Puerto Rico

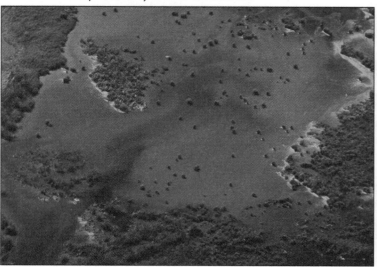

MINING FOR WATER

Surface water alone can't provide enough water for the human population. We get additional water by drawing it up from underground.

Water that you can see on the land, such as a pond or lake, is called surface water. A lot of water, however, is underground. This groundwater collects or flows through porous spaces in rocks, soil, and sediment. Geological formations that hold water are called aquifers. Most aquifers are made up of sand, sandstone, gravel, or fractured rock.

An aquifer can be close to the land's surface or quite deep. The top of the water level in an aquifer is called the water table. Below the water table, the ground is saturated with water. The water table separates the groundwater zone below it from the drier zone above it.

In some places, the water table might reach the surface in the form of a spring, oasis, river, or lake. In a swamp, the water table is often higher than the land surface—that's why the ground there is always damp and spongy.

A well is simply a hole dug down through the water table into the aquifer. If the water table is close to the ground surface, people can dig a well by hand and pull up water in a bucket! If the water table is deep, they use machinery to extract water.

Groundwater is often a cheaper and more convenient source of fresh water than surface water, partly because the United States has far more groundwater than surface water. In some areas, groundwater is the only option for part or all of the year. Groundwater is also less likely to get polluted than surface water. Public water supplies generally depend on groundwater.[17]

Mining is the removal of something from within the earth. Most often the term is used for the extraction of metals and minerals.

● ● ● ● ● ● ● ●

ROCK SOLID

Fossil water is water that has been stored in an aquifer for thousands of years. It cannot be replenished through current precipitation, so using this water lowers the water table.

TAKING AND GIVING

More than half of the people in the United States depend on groundwater for drinking and use in the home. Groundwater is also a major source of water for crop irrigation. Unfortunately, groundwater supplies are limited, so geologists are working to find ways of ensuring a good water supply for all.

Most groundwater comes from rain, melting snow, and ice. Water from these sources soaks into the ground to replenish the groundwater supplies. This process is called recharging the groundwater. The water table may rise after heavy rains or melting snow, but it's a slow process—in some areas, it can take a year or more to refill an aquifer just 1 inch.

> When people use groundwater faster than it is recharged, the water table falls.

A map of groundwater sites in the United States

credit: USGS

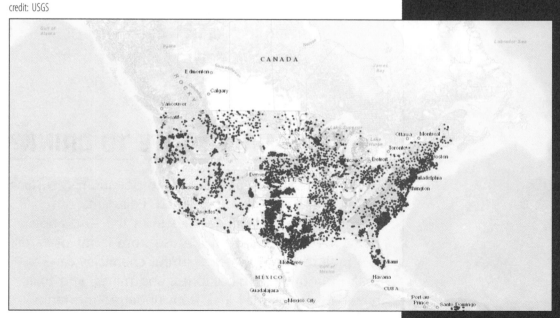

In the United States, the Ogallala Aquifer takes up more than 174,000 square miles beneath the Great Plains. It holds an enormous supply of groundwater and is one of the most important water sources in the country!

During the 1940s and 1950s, agriculture and development drained the aquifer faster than it could recharge. The water table dropped more than 3.5 feet a year. When a water table falls, the ground above it can subside to a lower level when soil collapses or is compressed. Fortunately, people came up with better irrigation practices, and the rate of draining slowed. In some areas, the water table even rose.

However, in most places, water is still being used at a much greater rate than the Ogallala Aquifer can recharge. By some estimates, people take about eight times more water from this aquifer than it gains. Much of that water goes to irrigating farm fields. Drought makes the situation even worse, and climate change is likely to bring more years of drought.

Geologists specializing in groundwater estimate that farmers in some areas may run out of water in 25 years if they keep using it at the current rate.[18]

IS YOUR WATER SAFE TO DRINK?

Groundwater is not as exposed to pollution as surface water, but it can still be polluted. Pollutants can sink into groundwater supplies from the land above. Heavy fertilizer and pesticide use from farms or yards can pollute groundwater. Harmful chemicals can soak in from landfills, factories, and mines, and toxic materials or gas may leak from underground tanks.

When water runs off of roads, it can carry any pollutants into the ground. This includes the salt spread on roads to melt ice in winter and chemical spills from accidents.

Pollution can even come from the septic tanks many people use to store and process human waste, if they are not properly planned and maintained. Household chemicals are another major source of groundwater pollution.

Salt water can also pollute fresh water. In coastal areas, pumping groundwater can cause salt water to move inland. It mixes with fresh water, turning the water brackish, or slightly salty. The salt level has to be reduced before the water is drinkable, and that process can be expensive.

Odd as it seems, the earth itself can pollute groundwater, too! Groundwater moves slowly through an aquifer—it can spend thousands of years in contact with the surrounding rock and sediment.

Minerals can dissolve into the groundwater, and even these natural substances can be harmful to humans.

HYDROLOGIST

Some geologists specialize in water. Hydrologists study the properties of surface fresh water while hydrogeologists study groundwater. Both study the complex water systems of the earth, advise communities on how to solve water problems, and help find safe water supplies. Hydrologists might study rainfall, snowpack, and river flows. They can map the land, study how water is currently being used, and advise communities on planning for future needs. Hydrologists often work to control river flooding or soil erosion or monitor a reservoir. Managing water can involve working with people across states and even between countries. Hydrologists also help protect the environment. They plan ways to clean up pollution, find sites for the safe disposal of hazardous wastes, and study the water quality in streams, rivers, and lakes. They may be the first ones to notice signs of a problem.

The world's first hydroelectric power plant began operating in 1882. It used the power of the Fox River in Wisconsin. By 1886, the United States and Canada had between 40 and 50 hydroelectric plants. The largest U.S. hydropower plant is on the Columbia River in Washington State.

WHEELING WATER

People have taken advantage of water power for more than 2,000 years. One early method involved using a waterwheel to saw wood or grind grain. A flowing river turned the wheel, which moved gears to do the work. Waterwheels even powered early factories, but they could only provide power close to the water source.

A water supply might naturally contain arsenic, mercury, copper, fluorine, or boron. These elements can sometimes build up to dangerous levels. Without proper water treatment, drinking water becomes poisonous. The technology to treat groundwater isn't always available in poor or undeveloped regions.

WATER POWER

People around the world use a lot of energy. Look around your room. How many things are using energy right now? Do you have a computer or laptop humming away? A smartphone? Electric lights? Did you get to school via a car, bus, or other type of transportation (other than a bike or on foot)? All of these things require energy to work.

Most electric power plants use steam to turn a turbine. As we learned in Chapter 2, many power plants burn coal or oil to heat water to make steam. Geothermal plants use heat from the earth to make steam. Hydroelectric power plants, on the other hand, don't need steam at all. They use moving water to turn the turbines. A hydroelectric plant changes the water's kinetic energy into electricity that can be carried long distances through wires.

> Hydroelectric power is considered renewable—it will never run out.

Hydroelectric plants also produce electricity at a fairly low cost. They release far fewer pollutants than power plants that use fossil fuels.

Most hydroelectric projects are built on large rivers, with dams installed to control the water. Above the dam, the water is stored in a reservoir that is often used for recreation.

From the dam, water is directed through a tunnel, where it turns a turbine, converting the kinetic energy of the moving water to mechanical energy. A generator converts the mechanical energy into electrical energy, and the water keeps flowing on down the river.

Does hydropower sound like a terrific clean energy solution? Hydropower has lots of benefits, along with some drawbacks. It's expensive to build new dams and power plants. Plus, damming a river to make a reservoir affects the surrounding environment. Sometimes, valleys upstream are flooded, destroying farms, towns, and wildlife habitat. The dam can block fish migration routes and the power plant can even change the water temperature, affecting local plants and animals.

For example, China built the Three Gorges Dam between 1994 and 2006 to gain a major source of power. The dam submerged parts of three gorges for hundreds of miles upstream, forcing 1.2 million people to move from their homes. Scientists warn that the reservoir sits on two major faults, so it could trigger severe earthquakes.

ROCK SOLID

Water can exist as a solid (ice or snow), liquid (water), and gas (water vapor). It is the only substance on Earth present in all three of these states of matter.

The Three Gorges Dam
credit: Gaynor (CC BY 2.0)

Take a tour of the Three Gorges Dam in this video!

 tour of Three Gorges Dam

They say that it is already responsible for several deadly landslides. The dam also threatens the biodiversity of plants and animals in the region. It has contributed to the further decline of an extremely rare dolphin.

Worldwide, hydropower supplies electricity to more than 1 billion people. It's expected to provide 16 percent of the world's electricity by 2023. That's more than wind, solar, or any other renewable energy source. In some countries, including Norway, Democratic Republic of the Congo, and Brazil, water provides more than 90 percent of the country's electricity. Canada gets about 60 percent of its electricity from hydropower.

The United States has more than 2,000 hydropower plants, yet it accounts for only 7 percent of total electricity. Most power in the United States comes from fossil fuels or nuclear power plants.

As of 2018, only 3 percent of the current dams in the United States are used to generate power. That means there's a lot of room for growth in hydropower, without incurring the cost of building new dams. The industry is growing and is expected to create more than 1.4 million jobs by 2025.

> Hydrologists will be well-suited to take some of these jobs. They can help ensure that hydropower is balanced with other water uses and environmental protection.

About 7.7 billion people in the world need fresh water. Hydrologists and other geologists help them get it. The science of geology has other ways of providing power. We'll take a look at more energy sources in the next chapter.[19]

VOCAB LAB

Write down what you think each word means. What root words can you find to help you? What does the context of the word tell you?

drought, **groundwater**, **hydroelectric**, **hydrology**, **renewable resource**, **saturate**, **water cycle**, and **water table**.

Compare your definitions with those of your friends or classmates. Did you all come up with the same meanings? Turn to the text and glossary if you need help.

Text-to-World Connection

● ● ● ● ● ● ● ● ●

Does your water come from a private well or a public system? Has it ever been tested for pollution?

KEY QUESTIONS

- **What are surface water and groundwater? Why is groundwater important?**
- **Can aquifers supply enough water for the future? Why or why not?**
- **How can pollution affect water supplies?**
- **What is hydroelectric power or hydropower? What are its pros and cons? What is its future potential?**

CONSERVE!

Conserving water helps ensure we will have enough for the future. Here are some ways your family can conserve water.

Turn off the water when brushing your teeth.

Take short showers rather than long showers or baths.

Fix leaky faucets, toilets, and showerheads.

Use low-flow shower heads and toilets.

Use high-efficiency dishwashers and clothes washers. Run full loads in the dishwasher and clothes washer.

Landscape with plants that need little water. Then water only when necessary.

Have a family meeting. Which of these are you already doing? Which might you like to try? How can you get started?

YOUR WATER USE

Think about all the ways you use water. Water conservation is a critical part of taking care of our planet. Take a good look at your own water usage and find ways to be more careful with your water use.

- **Track your water use throughout the day.** Make a note every time you turn on a faucet or flush a toilet. Make a note of other sources of water as well, such as canned or bottled beverages.

- **Research how much water is used for various activities.** The USGS provides some estimates here.

USGS home per capita

- **You can also try the 30by30 app from the Groundwater Foundation.** It is a free water-tracking app for Android and Apple devices.

- **How much water do you use every day?** Can you find instances throughout your day where you could cut back on water usage? What about the rest of your family? Can you be a positive force for change when it comes to water consumption?

To investigate more, consider that water is used to grow food as well. It is also used in manufacturing many of the objects around us. The U.S. Environmental Protection Agency includes these sources in its water use estimates.

EPA water use

Chapter 6 ▷
Feeding Our Energy Needs

STUDYING GEOLOGY CAN HELP US SAVE THE PLANET!

What is the connection between geology and energy?

Geologists work to find innovative ways of harnessing energy from different sources. Many geologists have an eye on curbing climate change and keeping the planet habitable.

● ● ● ● ● ● ● ● ●

Worldwide, the demand for energy is increasing. The world's population continues to rise and is expected to reach 9.6 billion by 2050. More people in developing countries are gaining access to technology that uses power, such as computers, televisions, and cars. In developed countries such as the United States, advertisers encourage people to buy more and more consumer goods—and manufacturing and transporting these products takes energy.

All of this means we can expect the demand for energy to keep growing.

Remember the fossil fuels that we dig out of the ground for energy? We discussed these briefly in earlier chapters. Let's take a closer look at coal, oil, and natural gas. These substances are called fossil fuels because they come from plants or animals that died long ago.

Coal is a solid that was created from plants that were squeezed under pressure for millions of years. Oil, or petroleum, is a liquid, often found alongside natural gas. Oil and natural gas formed from plants or tiny animals that lived in oceans. When these plants and animals died and sank to the bottom of the ocean, high pressure and high temperatures created chemical reactions that converted them to oil or gas. Today, petroleum may be found under the ocean floor or beneath land where ancient seas were located.

When coal is burned, it releases energy. Roughly 30 percent of the electricity in the United States starts with coal. Another 30 percent of the energy supply comes from natural gas. Gas can be converted to electricity or used directly for heating and cooking. Natural gas is used for making plastics and powers some public transportation vehicles.

Petroleum, also called crude oil, can be turned into gasoline to power vehicles. In the United States, more than 95 percent of all the energy used for transportation comes from oil. That means every year, America needs nearly 5 billion barrels of oil.

Bayswater Power Station in Australia

Learn more about petroleum with slides and diagrams from National Geographic.

 Nat Geo petroleum

THE LAW OF CONSERVATION OF ENERGY

Energy cannot be created or destroyed. It can change form, but the total amount of energy in the world always stays the same. Plants use the sun's energy to make food. Animals get energy by eating the plants or by eating other animals that ate plants. Millions of years ago, some of these plants and animals became fossil fuels, storing that energy. We burn the fuels to release the energy that originated with the sun. If energy can't be destroyed or created, why do we worry about running out? Because the energy that is stored in fossil fuels took billions of years to become usable, and once that coal or petroleum is used, it will take billions more years to return to that form.

Because fossil fuels are millions of years old and won't be replaced any time soon, the supply is limited. The sources of fossil fuels easiest to get have already been used, so companies are trying to drill deeper and find new sources.[20]

KEEPING THE ENERGY FLOWING

Many geologists work for the oil and gas industries. They help identify and map new sources of oil and gas. They might start by studying geologic maps. Then, they study and sample rock formations, looking for likely areas to explore based on the details of the rock. They use seismic data to get an idea of what's happening underground. All of this information helps them build geological models of the underground resource.

Maps and aerial photography provide more details that help geologists run computer simulations and develop plans. The geologists also assess the costs, benefits, and risks of tapping a resource. Then, the company might dig an exploration well or take core samples of the rock.

All this information tells geologists whether they have found a useful underground resource. If the reservoir is a good one, geologists make sure the company gets as much oil and gas out of the location as possible. They continue to monitor everything and identify risks in order to prevent accidents.

ROCK SOLID

In the nineteenth and early twentieth centuries, some streets and buildings used gaslight—lamps that burned natural gas.

Aerial satellite imagery of the Brahmani delta in eastern India

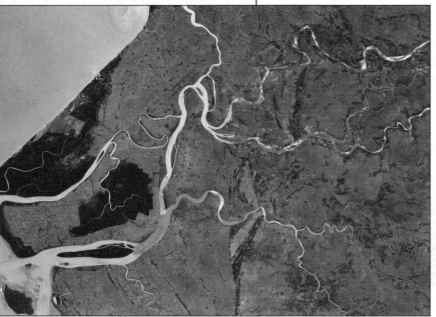

GETTING TO THE CORE OF THE MATTER

Geologists can learn a lot from looking at and mapping the landscape. They can find clues about the environment and climate that existed when the surface rock formed, and they can see how conditions changed with time by comparing older and younger rocks. They might find ancient fossils of animals and plants that show what species once lived there.

Yet, surface rocks do not provide a complete picture. Sometimes, a geologist is lucky enough to find a tall cliff wall that shows how rocks formed during the course of millions of years. But what about flatter land? What if the ground is covered by vegetation? What if the effects of weathering and erosion deposited a layer of sediment from elsewhere?

In those circumstances, the geologist can't see what's happening underground. But there's a way to dig deep without causing a huge disturbance!

Core samples allow scientists to see a continuous record of underground rock that might even go back millions of years.

A core sample is a section of sediment or rock extracted with a hollow steel tube called a core drill. Some of these drills are small enough for one person to move, but others are more like gigantic cranes. They can even be anchored on platforms in the ocean. Drills can cut down, up, horizontally, or at an angle, and can dig hundreds of feet down to take samples. A drill might work day and night for several days to take a sample that offers information stretching back millions of years.

OIL AND GAS SPECIALISTS

Like other geologists, oil and gas specialists might spend time in the field, in a lab, and in the office. A lot of time is spent analyzing data and preparing reports. Oil and gas specialists also work with other specialists, such as engineers and managers. Students interested in becoming oil and gas specialists often start by studying general geology. They might then focus on geophysics, geochemistry, or petroleum engineering. Jobs tend to be relatively plentiful and salaries fairly high. They can involve a lot of physical activity while working in the field. Oil companies also employ a variety of other experts. These companies need electricians, mechanics, accountants, lawyers, and designers.

See a video of a geologist describing her oil industry job at this website.

 Cat Burgess geophysicist

DRILLING DEEPER

The *Chikyu* research vessel is the world's deepest drill. It has reached 23,000 feet below the ocean floor, allowing scientists to study deep earthquake zones. By 2030, the drill will dig even farther—to reach through 2.5 miles of ocean and 3.7 miles of the earth's crust. Then, the plan is for it to drill 0.6 miles into the mantle to take samples. This will allow scientists to directly study the earth's mantle for the first time!

Core samples

ROCK SOLID

Usually, the oldest rock is at the bottom of the rock layers. But this can change if faults lift and turn some rock layers.

Whenever possible, the rock sample is preserved in sections several feet long, with the layers of rock and sediment matching what lies underground. Each section is carefully labeled to show how all the pieces fit together. With this information, geologists can estimate the size and quality of hidden resources, such as minerals or fossil fuels. Core samples can also help determine whether a site is suitable for buildings or dams.

Sometimes, core samples contain fossils, which show the prehistoric living things from an era.

Marine fossils, such as fish, might show that an area was once a marine setting, such as an ocean. Core samples can even include fossil pollen, which reveals the plants of the time. Fossils tell geologists when the rock was formed.[21]

ALTERNATIVE ENERGY

Some experts predict that the world could run out of fossil fuels by the year 2050. What are we to do?

New technologies might help us find more sources of fossil fuels, but these will likely be in deeper or more remote locations, which means it will cost more to access them. In addition, burning fossil fuels releases carbon dioxide (CO_2) and other polluting gases. These greenhouse gases act like a blanket over the earth, trapping energy that warms the earth's surface. Greenhouse gases increase the effects of climate change, leading to more heat waves, droughts, and dramatic storms.

The pollutants released by using fossil fuels are bad for human health. They can irritate the lungs and lead to bronchitis, pneumonia, and other respiratory infections. The pollution combines with rain to create acid rain, which can damage buildings and harm the soil where we grow food. Fossil fuel mining and transportation can also poison water sources.

> The Union of Concerned Scientists recommends that we shift away from fossil fuels and focus on cleaner, renewable sources of energy.

Fortunately, we have several options for renewable energy resources. We've already discussed geothermal and hydroelectric power. There's also tidal power, which uses the energy of waves and tides. Such power plants are not common, however, because they must be able to withstand powerful ocean storms. Biomass uses organic matter, such as plants that can be regrown, as fuel. Solar power and wind power are also forms of renewable energy.

GROUND PENETRATION

Ground penetrating radar (GPR) is another way of seeing into the ground. GPR sends a tiny pulse of energy into the ground and records the reflected signal. Different materials reflect the signal at different strengths and times. Some materials allow the signal to partially pass through, while others do not. For example, metal does not allow signals to pass through. Dry sand, wet sand, and limestone rock all return different signals. This data helps geologists understand what materials are below the ground. GPR can only reach depths of up to 100 feet at best. Other techniques allow geologists to see farther into the earth. One method, seismic reflection, creates vibrations. The reflected energy waves are recorded and processed to create a visual representation of the structures underground.

See a video from the oil and gas company OMV explaining seismic reflection.

 OMV: What is seismic reflection?

Renewable energy is energy that can be easily replaced. The wind and the sun will always be there!

Most forms of alternative energy depend on the geology of a location. Geothermal energy needs underground geothermal resources, while hydropower requires flowing water and a certain type of landscape. Solar and wind power farms need sites that are suitable and stable.

Even after the renewable power is captured, that power still must be transferred to users through electric power lines. Once again, the landscape plays a huge role! Geography determines how easy or difficult it is to set up and maintain power lines, and geologists may survey the land to find the best sites for each type of energy. They can also assess how energy development will affect the climate, local water resources, and ecosystems.

ROCK SOLID

Even renewable resources require mining to build the pieces. For example, wind turbines and solar panels are built largely of metals.

A wind farm

The Krafla geothermal power plant in Iceland

POWER FROM THE ATOM

Nuclear power is another form of alternative energy. This type of power splits atoms in order to create nuclear reactions. The reactions release nuclear energy and generate heat. In the United States, almost 20 percent of electricity comes from nuclear energy. It is also an important source of energy in many other countries.

Nuclear power has some major risks, however. Running a nuclear power plant does not pollute the air, but it does produce hazardous waste. In addition, nuclear energy requires uranium, a radioactive metal. Mining uranium can pollute the land and water if the waste rock is not properly handled. In the United States, the Environmental Protection Agency regulates and monitors uranium mining, but those regulations do not exist in many less developed countries. Nuclear power plants must be built on stable ground that is not prone to earthquakes or tsunamis.

Nuclear waste remains dangerous for thousands of years, and, therefore, requires a safe, underground site for long-term storage. Some geologists help to identify suitable sites—but most people don't want nuclear waste in their region. The disposal of nuclear waste is a big and expensive challenge.

ROCK SOLID

Weather is temperature, cloudiness, rainfall, and wind—what we experience day to day. Climate is the average weather in an area during a long period of time. An area might have unusually cold weather even though the climate is warming on average.

Watch a video about how carbon releases its energy and why that contributes to global warming. What is the connection between carbon and material wealth?

 NPR carbon video

A CHANGING CLIMATE

One of the key concerns of our time is climate change. The geological record shows how the earth's climate has changed in the past and how these changes affected animal and plant life. This record also provides scientific evidence for the changes that are caused by human activities. It helps geologists understand how climate may change in the future.

When glaciers scrape over the ground, they create a distinctive mixed sediment called till. Where geologists find till, they know that, in the past, it was cold enough for a glacier. Rocks formed in a hot desert environment are often red with iron deposits. Salt can be another indicator of a previous hot or dry climate—seawater evaporates more quickly at high temperatures, often leaving behind a layer of salt that gets preserved in the rock.

Fossils also show what the climate was like when the rock formed, as species adapt to the local landscape. You wouldn't expect to find lizards and polar bears in the same location!

Current scientific study shows that the earth is now suffering from what's called the greenhouse effect. This happens when gases and substances in the atmosphere trap the sun's radiation. The trapped radiation makes the earth warmer, on average. Global warming is one example of the greenhouse effect.

Several pollutants contribute to the greenhouse effect. The most important is CO_2. Volcano eruptions release CO_2. So does breathing! Humans and other organisms take in air, use oxygen, and release carbon dioxide. When organisms die and decompose, they also release CO_2. When limestone rock is exposed to weathering, CO_2 is released. We have little control over carbon dioxide being released in these ways.

Because all these factors have been around for millions of years, they do not explain the current warming trend. Most climate scientists agree that human activity is the main cause of the current change in climate, and see its beginning during the Industrial Revolution. Cities and factories started to replace small towns and farming, and factories and industry rely heavily on fossil fuels and wood—all of which release carbon dioxide when burned.

Cutting down forests can also contribute to climate change. Trees use CO_2 for photosynthesis, so they reduce the amount of CO_2 in the atmosphere. Fewer trees means more carbon dioxide.

As the earth becomes warmer on average, some regions become wetter, while others become drier. Plants and animals may no longer be able to survive in their traditional habitats. While some might be able to move to new areas, others will die out.

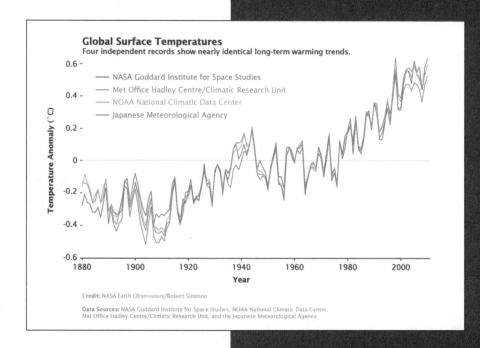

Global Surface Temperatures
Four independent records show nearly identical long-term warming trends.

— NASA Goddard Institute for Space Studies
— Met Office Hadley Centre/Climatic Research Unit
— NOAA National Climatic Data Center
— Japanese Meteorological Agency

Credit: NASA Earth Observatory/Robert Simmon

Data Sources: NASA Goddard Institute for Space Studies, NOAA National Climatic Data Center, Met Office Hadley Centre/Climatic Research Unit, and the Japanese Meteorological Agency.

HUMAN VS. VOLCANO

Volcanoes bring gases such as carbon dioxide from the depths of the earth to the surface. Yet, human activities may generate more than 130 times the amount of CO_2 emitted by volcanoes. Volcanoes also release ash particles, which can block the sun's rays and temporarily lower global temperatures. So, volcanoes can both warm and cool the planet in the short term. Human activity is only warming it.

Text-to-World Connection

● ● ● ● ● ● ●

What can you do to help with the problem of climate change?

Because life on Earth is so interrelated, whenever one species is affected, others are, too. People are suffering as well. Some areas are more prone to droughts, flooding, or other extreme weather. Crops can be destroyed, farm animals may die, and people may starve.

On a warming planet, glaciers and the polar ice sheets melt faster, which causes sea levels to rise. Ocean water also expands as it warms, further contributing to a rising sea level. Coastal communities, and even whole islands, may be flooded and millions of people could lose their homes. More species will die out because warm water reefs and Arctic ecosystems are especially vulnerable to climate change.

Fortunately, we do have some control over human activities. We can make choices that affect global climate change.[22]

Boulder Glacier in Washington State. You can see how much the glacier has retreated since 1985.

GEOLOGY TO THE RESCUE

Many geologists are working to solve the problem of climate change. They are developing a more detailed and accurate understanding of the situation, and they are working to improve alternative energies.

Some geologists are involved with trying to remove CO_2 from the atmosphere. This process is called carbon capture and storage (CCS). CCS captures CO_2 from large emission sources, such as power plants, then transports and stores it deep underground. Geologists determine suitable underground formations for storage.

CCS is relatively new, but test sites have shown that the technology works. This could become an important way of limiting the release of greenhouse gases. Right now, CCS is expensive, but new advances could make it more affordable.

> If power plants that use fossil fuels start using CCS, they could reduce CO_2 emissions by about 80 to 90 percent.

Geologists can also help people adapt to the changing climate by predicting how flooding patterns will change, how droughts will stress water supplies, and how rising seawater might affect coastal fresh water. They monitor water supplies and advise communities on how to adapt. Finally, geologists can help predict future changes by using complex mathematical and computer models.

Maybe someday, we will be able to produce all the energy people want without polluting the planet. In the meantime, geologists can help provide the energy and address the problems its use creates.

VOCAB LAB

Write down what you think each word means. What root words can you find to help you? What does the context of the word tell you?

core sample, **fossil fuels**, **global warming**, **greenhouse effect**, **Industrial Revolution**, **nuclear power**, and **till**.

Compare your definitions with those of your friends or classmates. Did you all come up with the same meanings? Turn to the text and glossary if you need help.

KEY QUESTIONS

- **How much do we depend on fossil fuels? What will it take for people to change their energy habits?**

- **How are geologists important to the discovery and invention of climate change solutions?**

MAP YOUR SCHOOLYARD OR NEIGHBORHOOD

Maps are crucial in the study of geology. A good way to learn about maps is to make a map of a familiar area. Choose a fairly small location, such as your schoolyard, an outdoor shopping area, or a few city blocks.

- **Start by studying other maps.** Get several of different scales and designs for different purposes.

  - What do they include?
  - Do they show only streets?
  - Do they show natural formations?
  - Do they show elevation changes?

- **You can trace a map of the area you chose or draw it freehand.** You can also print an aerial image of the area from the National Geologic Map Database at this website.

 Nat Geo map database

- **Determine what colors you want to use for different objects.** Buildings might be one color, grass another. Add all the elements you want in your map. Why do you want to include these? What information are you trying to relay to the end user?

- **Make a legend for your map.** A legend explains what each color means and indicates directions.

- **Add the map scale.** Find a feature that will be easy to measure, such as a yard or parking space. Measure it with a tape measure. Measure the feature on your map with a ruler. Determine the scale and add it to your map.

To investigate more, explore the area your map covers. Note what kind of geological features are present. How big should a rock be before it goes on your map? You might include individual large boulders. But a gravel yard might be better marked with a special color to indicate gravel.

For photo examples of stone buildings, and the types of stone used, visit the department of geology at University of Georgia.

 UGA stone gallery

Chapter 7 ▶
The Changing Science of Geology

THE ANCIENT PAST HAS A BIG IMPACT ON OUR FUTURE, TOO!

What can we learn with geology?

BY DISCOVERING HOW THINGS HAVE HAPPENED IN THE PAST . . .

. . . WE CAN PREDICT HOW AND WHEN THEY'LL HAPPEN IN THE FUTURE!

THAT WAY, THERE'S LESS DAMAGE FROM NATURAL DISASTERS AND WE CAN EVEN PROTECT NATURE!

Geology is a science that touches on many other sciences and industries, including geography, cartography, even astronomy!

● ● ● ● ● ● ● ●

The field of geology has changed in many ways since it was first established. Theories have been developed and refined as new information is uncovered on a regular basis. Sometimes, discoveries even change our understanding of our planet's history.

As with any science, geology is shaped and reshaped on a constant basis according to new discoveries. We can see this happen as geologists have tried to answer the age-old question, "How old is Earth?"

Before scientific inquiry and evidence-based conclusions became standard practices, people looked toward stories for answers. Many believed that the Bible proved the earth was only about 6,000 years old. But, as geology became a more and more advanced field of study, people used science to answer the question of how old the earth is.

Let's take a look at how.

AS OLD AS THE EARTH

To help figure out the answer to the age of the earth, geologists have dated rock samples. How do scientists determine the age of a rock? Relative dating puts geologic events in chronological order, but does not determine the age of each event. For example, a cliff wall may show horizontal layers, called strata. In general, the layers on the bottom were deposited first, and, therefore, are older than the layers on top. This can change due to the movement of faults or other geologic forces, but those events also leave traces in the rock record.

Absolute dating estimates the age of geological materials such as rocks or fossils. Scientists discovered radioactivity in 1896. During the next half-century, they found a way to use radioactivity to date rocks. Chemical elements in rocks have slightly different forms, known as isotopes. Some isotopes are unstable—they slowly and steadily change into different isotopes.

For example, uranium 238 decays into lead during hundreds of millions of years. This process is called radioactive decay. The rate of decay is constant and predictable for each isotope. Using a process called radiometric dating, scientists can measure the ratio of uranium to lead in a rock sample to learn the rock's age.

ROCK SOLID

Radiometric dating found moon rock samples to be about 4.5 million years old.

Strata in a cliff face

Astronomy helps confirm the age of the planet. Astronomers believe the sun to be about 4.6 billion years old. Asteroids have been dated to 4.5 billion years old. It's likely that the earth formed around that time.

As Old As . . .

In 2017, a Japanese team said it had dated a set of fossils as 3.95 billion years old. Most scientists still state that life on Earth is about 3.5 billion years old. Yet, every few years, a headline announces that life on Earth is even older than previously thought. It seems likely that the age will keep changing slightly as new information is found and our technology gets better.

So, how does this help geologists determine the age of the earth? Zircon crystals found in the Australian desert have been dated to 4.375 billion years. These crystals started forming after the earth formed, so the earth is older than the crystals.

Could the earth be even older than current estimates say? If geologists find older geological material, they will update the estimated age. One of the amazing things about science is that there is always the possibility for new evidence to reveal new information.

Another big question that scientists try to answer is, "How long has life been on Earth?" Geologists look for evidence in rocks. They have found microfossils, too small to see with the naked eye, from bacteria and microbes. Some of these fossils have been dated to almost 3.5 billion years ago.

However, scientists don't always agree on how to interpret data. For example, in 2016, scientists identified material from an ancient seafloor as microbial fossils and dated the samples as 3.7 billion years old. But NASA studied the structures and decided they were probably not fossils at all. The original scientists defended their claim. Who's right? Did life on Earth start 3.5 billion years ago or 3.7 billion years ago?

BETTER MAPPING

Another area where technology makes a difference is cartography, or mapmaking. Early maps were only roughly accurate. Geographers sketched in features based on what they saw or what other travelers reported. This led to lots of missing sections! A map designed for sea traders might show an accurate coastline but ignore anything inland.

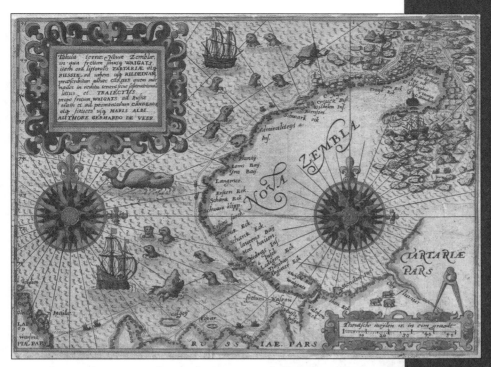

A map of the Northeast Passage (now in the Russian Arctic) drawn in 1601 by Theodore de Bry

Mapmaking techniques have greatly improved since those days. Scientists began to estimate locations on land based on the location of objects in space. They estimated the circumference of the planet using math. As people explored more of the world, geographers filled in the gaps on maps.

The invention of Global Positioning System (GPS) made maps even more accurate and detailed.

Geologists with a GPS no longer have to estimate distances. They can plot points or paths with great accuracy. Have you ever used GPS on a car trip? It's pretty useful and very different from the days when sea monsters appeared on maps to indicate unknown areas!

FLAT MAPPING

It's hard to map the earth, which is a sphere, accurately on a flat surface such as paper. A globe is more accurate because it mimics the spherical shape of the planet. Map design is constantly evolving. Learn more about the history of cartography at this website.

 mapping through ages GIS

Artist's impression of a GPS satellite in orbit

ROCK SOLID

Car GPS systems and smartphones combine GPS data with maps. Using this information, they can give directions and estimate the time of arrival.

GPS depends on receiving information from special satellites that orbit the earth. The satellites contain a computer, a clock, and a radio. Each satellite constantly broadcasts its position and time. The satellites are spaced so that every point on Earth should be able to read signals from at least four satellites.

GPS receivers on the ground get location information from the satellites. With data from at least three of the satellites, they can determine the position of the GPS device. They know the latitude, or the distance of a place north or south of the earth's equator. They can also pinpoint the longitude, the east-west position of the place. If the receiver has a map, it can show the device's position. With a signal from a fourth satellite, the receiver can also figure out the altitude. By taking readings as a GPS device moves, the speed and direction of travel can also be calculated.

Many GPS devices are accurate within 10 meters of most locations. Special military satellites are accurate to 1 meter. They can tell what part of the room you are in![23]

DRONES

Satellites can take pictures from space, which allows programs such as Google Earth to build worldwide maps that even show terrain and buildings in 3-D. Have you spent time looking at Google Earth?

Satellites take pictures from far away, while planes and helicopters can take aerial pictures from closer to the ground. Now, there's a way to get even closer. Unmanned aircraft systems (UAS) are more commonly known as drones. In technical terms, a drone is any aerial vehicle that does not include a person on board.

Before 2006, most drones were used for military purposes. Now, drones are used by hobbyists, schools, businesses, filmmakers—anyone! Drones are small and maneuverable and have gotten cheaper, fancier, and much more common. They can move in any direction, hover in place, and can be mounted with equipment to take photographs, videos, or measurements. They fly close to the ground, so their photographs are very detailed.

To make maps, drones typically take overlapping photos in a grid pattern. Points are matched between overlapping images. Then, latitude, longitude, and elevation of different points is calculated. Drones can take photos of features from multiple angles to help scientists understand and map the features more accurately.

> Geologists use drones in the field to get a better look at landforms.

The machines can fly through canyons that might be impossible for a hiker or aircraft to go through. They can safely monitor dangerous sinkholes, areas prone to landslides, volcanoes, earthquake epicenters, and other places that are too dangerous for humans.

Drones even help geologists learn more about geologic processes. The machines can fly over the same geologic feature repeatedly to see how it changes with time.

ROCK SOLID

In 1839, Austrian soldiers attacked the city of Venice with balloons filled with explosives. This is the earliest known unmanned aerial vehicle. During World War II, radio-controlled drones were used for military purposes. Later, the United States and the Soviet Union (now Russia) used drones to spy on each other.

FORENSIC GEOLOGY

Who's been polluting the lake? That's a question forensic geologists can help answer. When an area is polluted, forensic geologists can determine how old the contaminants are. Was it the current landowner or a previous one? Who should be responsible for cleaning up a site?

Were people exposed to chemicals in the soil or water where they work or live? A forensic geologist can find out and help determine who is responsible for the chemicals. Knowing what or who is responsible helps determine who should pay for the damage and how to prevent the situation in the future. Forensic geologists can even help with crime scene investigation. When two objects come into contact, material is transferred between them, including soil, rocks, minerals, and water. A forensic geologist determines where the material came from.

Geologists can use drones to study landslides, rock falls, and mudflows. They can see how rivers and streams alter their paths and can track the effects of erosion in detail.[24]

Mining companies use drones for mineral or petroleum exploration. Drones can monitor hazardous areas, so people are not put at risk. When mounted with thermal cameras and equipment that senses gases, drones can look for natural gas leaks, which saves money and protects the environment.

Geologists also use their own feet, hands, and eyes to visit sites and get information firsthand. Another tool they use is a geographic information system (GIS). GIS is a tool that helps mappers present the information they have gathered. GIS can show data as a 2-D map or even as a 3-D scene.

A visual representation of data in a geographic information system

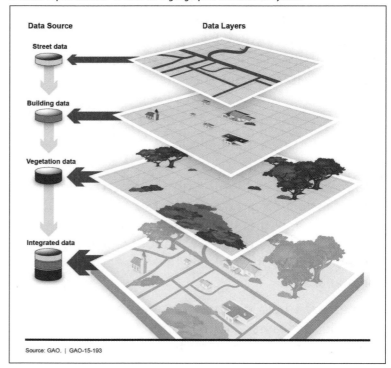

Source: GAO. | GAO-15-193

A map can be adjusted to show many different things, such as geologic faults or sources of pollution alongside water supplies. GIS makes it easier for geologists to build maps that other people can easily understand.

GIS is used in many fields today. City planners need GIS specialists to help plan and improve neighborhoods. Mining and petroleum companies use GIS to find mineral or oil and gas resources. Health geographers use GIS to track diseases and stop them from spreading. Helicopter firefighters use GIS to study fires from the air and plan how to fight the fire more effectively. Climate scientists combine GIS and climate data to understand how our planet is changing.

Geology is a vast science with many applications and a wide variety of career opportunities. In its simplest definition, geology is the study of the history, structure, and origin of the earth through its rocks. Being a geologist includes an enormous variety of research areas, jobs, and interests.

The next time you walk down a city street or through the woods, look at the geological clues around you. What could be happening under your feet? The clues are there, waiting for a geological detective to find.

KEY QUESTIONS

- **How and why does our knowledge of geology change through time?**
- **How has mapping improved in recent years?**
- **How does GPS help create more accurate maps?**

Text-to-World Connection

● ● ● ● ● ● ● ● ●

Has GPS ever surprised you during a trip? How?

UNDERSTANDING YOUR NEIGHBORHOOD

Go on a neighborhood walk and see what you can learn with your new geological knowledge. How does the environment affect your community? How does your community affect the environment?

- **If you have a GPS device or GPS in a phone, use it to determine the location of your observations.** Take a photo and record notes at each location. Many apps can help you map these points.

- **What can you determine about the ages of things you see?** For example, which is older, a building or the bricks used to make the building? Does a sidewalk show signs of cracks or repairs that came after the sidewalk was poured? Can you find records of "absolute" ages, such as dates stamped on manhole covers or plaques on buildings?

- **Can you determine the effects of weathering or erosion on buildings, streets, or the landscape?** What do these effects look like?

- **Study maps of your neighborhood.** How does a street map differ from a Google Earth map that shows the terrain or a 3-D image? Which map is best for someone trying to find an address? What are the best uses for the other maps? What would you include if you wanted to make a map for someone who just moved there?

To investigate more, imagine you are a city planner. What changes would you make to your neighborhood? Is there room for more growth? Should streets be widened? Should sidewalks or bike lanes be added or expanded? How would you balance different uses?

abrasion: wearing, grinding, or rubbing away by friction.

abrasive: a grainy substance.

absolute dating: the process of determining a specific age or order of events.

acid rain: precipitation that has been polluted by acid.

aerial: something that is in or has to do with the air.

aftershock: an earthquake that happens after the initial shock.

age: a distinct period of history or prehistory, which in geology may last millions of years.

agriculture: the practice of farming, including growing crops and raising animals to provide food and other products.

amateur: someone who is not a professional.

aquifer: a layer of sand, gravel, and rock that has pores or openings through which groundwater flows.

Archean eon: one of the four geologic eons of earth history, occurring 4 to 2.5 billion years ago.

asphalt: a black tar that is used to pave roads.

atom: a small particle of matter. Atoms are the extremely tiny building blocks of everything.

avalanche: a massive movement of snow or rocks down a mountain or slope.

bacteria: microorganisms found in soil, water, plants, and animals that are sometimes harmful but often helpful.

basalt: a black, shiny volcanic rock.

biodiversity: the range of living things in an area.

biomass: biological material that can be used as fuel or as an energy source.

brackish: slightly salty water that is a mix of seawater and river water.

canyon: a deep trench in the earth, often with steep sides.

carbon capture and storage (CCS): the process of trapping carbon dioxide and storing it, usually in an underground geological formation, so it cannot affect the atmosphere.

cartography: the art and science of making maps.

chemical formula: a set of chemical symbols showing the elements in a compound.

chemical weathering: the erosion of rocks, building materials, etc., caused by chemical reactions. These reactions typically come from water and substances dissolved in it.

cinder cone volcano: a steep cone-shaped hill around a volcanic vent, typically formed by explosive eruptions.

circumference: the distance around the outside of a circle or globe.

climate: the average weather patterns in an area during a long period of time.

climate change: a change in long-term weather patterns, which can happen through natural or manmade processes.

collapse earthquakes: small earthquakes underground and in mines caused by seismic waves from the surface, which may cause the roof of the mine or cavern to collapse.

composite volcano: also known as a stratovolcano, a cone-shaped volcano built up of many layers of hardened lava, pumice, and ash.

compress: to flatten by pressure.

contaminate: to pollute or make dirty.

continent: one of the earth's major land masses.

continental drift: the gradual movement of the continents across the earth's surface through geological time.

core: the central part of something.

convection current: a current in a fluid, such as molten rock, that transfers heat from one place to another by motion.

convergent boundary: in plate tectonics, a boundary between two tectonic plates that are moving toward each other.

core sample: a section from deep within something, such as a tree or glacier, that is taken by drilling for scientific investigation.

GLOSSARY

crater: a large hole in the ground caused by the impact of something such as a piece of an asteroid, a bomb, or volcanic debris.

crust: the earth's outer layer.

crystal: a solid where the atoms are arranged in a highly ordered pattern.

debris: scattered pieces of something wrecked or destroyed.

deposition: the geological process in which sediments, soil, and rocks are added to land.

detonation: the action of causing an explosive device to explode.

dilute: to make something weaker by adding other elements to it.

divergent boundary: in plate tectonics, a boundary between two tectonic plates that are moving away from each other.

dormant volcano: a volcano that is still capable of erupting, but hasn't for a long time.

downcut: to erode downward, as in a river cutting down through its bed.

drone: an unmanned aerial vehicle.

drought: a long period of unusually low rainfall that can harm plants and animals.

duration: the time during which something continues.

earthquake: a sudden movement in a piece of the outer layer of the earth. It releases stress built up from the motion of the earth's plates.

ecosystem: a community of living and nonliving things and their environment. Living things are plants, animals, and insects. Nonliving things are soil, rocks, and water.

elevation: the height of something above sea level.

engineering: the use of science and math in the design and construction of machines and structures.

environmental: relating to the natural world and the impact of human activity on its condition.

eon: a billion years or more.

epicenter: the point on the earth's surface directly above the origin of an earthquake.

epoch: in geology, a division of time smaller than a period and larger than an age.

era: in geology, a division of time that is smaller than an eon and larger than a period. Eras typically last hundreds of millions of years.

erosion: the gradual wearing away of rock or soil by water and wind.

eruption: a violent explosion of gas, steam, or ash.

ethical: acting in a way that upholds someone's belief in right and wrong.

evacuate: to move a person from one place to another as a protective measure.

evaporation: the process by which a liquid becomes a gas.

evolution: the process of living things gradually changing to adapt to the world around them.

explosion earthquake: an earthquake caused by nuclear or chemical devices exploding.

extinct volcano: a volcano that doesn't have magma anymore and therefore won't erupt again.

extract: to remove or take out by effort or force.

famine: a period of great hunger and lack of food for a large population of people.

fault line: a fracture in the earth's crust. Major fault lines form the boundaries between the tectonic plates.

fertile: land that is rich in nutrients and good for growing crops.

forensic: applying scientific methods to investigate a crime.

foreshock: a tremor that happens before the primary seismic shock of an earthquake.

fossil: the remains or traces of ancient plants or animals left in rock.

fossil fuels: fuels made from the remains of plants and animals that lived millions of years ago. Coal, oil, and natural gas are fossil fuels.

fossil water: an ancient body of water that has been undisturbed for thousands of years.

fracking (hydraulic fracturing): the process of injecting liquid into underground rocks at high pressure in order to force open existing cracks.

galvanize: to shock or excite someone into taking action.

gem: a precious or semiprecious stone valued for jewelry or other ornamentation.

generator: a device that turns motion into electricity.

geochemistry: a science that studies the chemical composition of and chemical changes in the solid matter of the earth or a celestial body.

geographer: a person who studies the earth's surface and its people, plants, and animals.

Geographic Information System (GIS): a system designed to capture, store, analyze, and present geographical data of all types.

geologic timescale: the way time is divided into large blocks to describe the 4.6-billion-year history of the earth.

geologist: a scientist who studies geology, which is the history, structure, and origin of the earth and its rocks.

geology: the study of the history, structure, and origin of the earth and its rocks.

geophysics: a branch of earth science dealing with the physics of the earth.

geothermal energy: energy from below the surface of the earth. It can heat and cool by using differences in temperature between a structure and the earth.

geyser: a hot spring that periodically ejects water and steam in the air.

glacier: a huge sheet of ice and snow.

Global Positioning System (GPS): a system of satellites, computers, and receivers that can determine the exact location of a receiver anywhere on the planet.

global warming: a gradual increase in the average temperature of the earth's atmosphere and its oceans.

gravity: a physical force that draws everything toward the center of the earth.

greenhouse effect: a process through which energy from the sun is trapped by a planet's atmosphere, warming the planet.

greenhouse gas: a gas such as water vapor, carbon dioxide, or methane that traps heat and contributes to warming temperatures.

ground penetrating radar (GPR): a tool that uses radar pulses to create images of what exists below the earth's surface.

groundwater: underground water found in aquifers.

habitable: capable of supporting life.

habitat: the natural area where a plant or animal lives.

Hadean eon: a geologic period that began with the formation of the earth about 4.6 billion years ago and ended 4 billion years ago.

hazardous: risky or dangerous.

heavy metal: a metal that is very dense, especially one that is poisonous, such as lead and mercury.

Homo sapiens: the species to which all modern human beings belong.

hot spot: a volcanic region where hot plumes rise from the earth's mantle to the surface.

hydraulic fracturing: the process of injecting liquid into underground rocks at high pressure in order to force open existing cracks.

hydroelectric: electricity generated from the energy of flowing water.

hydrology: the branch of geology focused on the study of water. A hydrologist is a scientist who studies the earth's water.

ice wedging: a form of mechanical weathering in which cracks fill with water, freeze, and expand, causing the cracks to enlarge and eventually break.

igneous rock: rock formed through the cooling and solidification of magma or lava.

indigenous: native to a place.

Industrial Revolution: a period during the eighteenth and nineteenth centuries when large cities began to replace small towns and farming and people started using machines to make things in large factories.

inorganic: not part of the living world, such as metal and glass.

intensity: the strength, power, or force of something.

interpret: to think about something and explain it.

irrigation: a system of transporting water through canals or tunnels to water crops.

isotope: a variation of an atom. Isotopes of an atom have the same number of protons but different numbers of neutrons.

kinetic energy: energy caused by an object's motion.

GLOSSARY

landform: a natural feature of the earth's surface, such as a mountain or river.

landscape: a large area of land and its features, such as mountains and rivers.

landslide: the sliding down of a large mass of earth or rock from a cliff or mountain.

latitude: a measure of distance from the equator, in degrees. The equator is 0 degrees. The North Pole is 90 degrees latitude north and the South Pole is 90 degrees latitude south.

lava: hot, melted rock that has risen to the surface of the earth.

lava bomb: a mass of molten rock larger than 2.5 inches in diameter formed when a volcano ejects fragments of lava during an eruption.

lava dome: a roughly circular mound resulting from lava that has been slowly released from a volcanic vent.

leaching: a process by which substances are washed out from soil.

lidar: Light Detection and Ranging, a surveying method that uses laser light to measure distances.

liquefaction: the process of making something liquid.

lithosphere: the hard and rigid outer part of the earth, consisting of the crust and upper mantle.

longitude: a measure of distance from the prime meridian, in degrees. The prime meridian is 0 degrees with lines running 180 degrees east and west from it.

magma: a mixture of molten, semi-molten, and solid rock beneath Earth's surface.

magnitude: the measurement of the strength of an earthquake.

mantle: the layer of the earth between the crust and core. The upper mantle, together with the crust, forms the lithosphere.

mechanical energy: the ability to do work, associated with the motion and position of an object. Mechanical energy is the sum of potential energy and kinetic energy.

mechanical weathering: the process through which large rocks are broken into smaller pieces through mechanical processes, such as tree roots growing in cracks.

metamorphic rock: a type of rock that has been changed by extreme heat and pressure.

meteorite: a meteor that is not burned up by the earth's atmosphere and hits the earth's surface.

microbe: a living organism that can be seen only with a microscope, such as bacteria. Also called a microorganism.

migration: moving from one place to another, often with the change in seasons.

mineral: a naturally occurring solid found in rocks and in the ground. Rocks are made of minerals. Gold and diamonds are precious minerals.

mining: taking minerals, such as iron ore, from the ground.

molecule: a group of atoms bonded together, the simplest structural unit of an element or compound. Molecules can break apart and form new ones, which is a chemical reaction.

molten: melted by heat to a liquid.

natural disaster: a natural event, such as a fire or flood, that causes great damage to a human population.

nuclear power: energy produced when the nucleus of an atom is split apart.

oasis: a green area with water in a dry region or desert. The plural of oasis is oases.

obsidian: black volcanic glass formed by the rapid cooling of lava.

organic matter: decaying plants and animals that give soil its nutrients.

organism: a living thing, such as a plant or animal.

oxidation: the loss or transfer of electrons.

ozone layer: the layer of the earth's atmosphere that contains ozone and blocks the sun's ultraviolet rays.

paleontologist: a scientist who studies paleontology, the study of the fossils of plants and animals.

paleoseismology: the study of prehistoric earthquakes that have been preserved in the geologic record.

Pangaea: a huge supercontinent that existed about 200 million years ago. It contained all the land on Earth.

period: in geology, a division of time smaller than an era and larger than an epoch.

perlite: a natural volcanic glass with a lightweight form that may be used in soil for potted plants, in fire-resistant insulation, and for other uses.

pesticide: a substance used to destroy pests harmful to people, animals, or plants.

petroleum: a thick, dark liquid that occurs naturally beneath the earth. It can be separated into many products, including gasoline and other fuels and plastics.

photosynthesis: the process a plant goes through to make its own food. The plant uses water and carbon dioxide in the presence of sunlight to make oxygen and sugar.

plastic deformation: a permanent change in shape caused by stress.

plate tectonics: the theory that describes how plates in the earth's crust slowly move and interact with each other to produce earthquakes, volcanoes, and mountains.

plateau: a large, raised area of land that is fairly flat and often cut by deep canyons.

pollutant: a substance that is harmful to the environment.

porous: full of many little holes so water passes through.

primary waves: the fastest moving seismic waves. They can travel through solids, liquids, and gases and may cause rocks to change in volume.

processor: the part of a computer that interprets and exchanges information.

projectile: an object that is thrown.

pumice: a light rock full of air spaces, formed from solidified lava.

pyroclastic flow: the current of lava and dirt that spreads out along the ground from a volcano after an eruption.

radioactivity: the emission of a stream of particles or electromagnetic rays.

radiometric dating: a method of determining the age of rocks. It looks at a radioactive element in rock, such as uranium, and measures how much it has decayed.

recharge: the filling of an aquifer by absorbing more water.

relative dating: the science of determining the order of past events, without necessarily determining their specific age.

renewable resource: a resource that cannot be used up, such as solar energy.

reservoir: a large natural or artificial lake used as a water supply.

resource: something that people can use, such as water, food, and building materials.

Richter scale: a scale for measuring the strength of earthquakes.

Ring of Fire: a geographical area around the edges of the Pacific Ocean, which has high volcanic and seismic activity.

rock: a naturally occurring solid made up of minerals.

runoff: produced when water picks up wastes as it flows over the surface of the ground. Runoff can pollute streams, lakes, rivers, and oceans.

satellite: a device that orbits the earth to relay communication signals or transmit information.

saturate: to soak with water.

scale: a measuring system.

secondary waves: the second fastest traveling seismic waves, after primary waves. Secondary waves can travel through solids, but not through liquids or gases.

sediment: bits of rock, sand, or dirt that have been carried to a place by water, wind, or a glacier.

sedimentary rock: rock formed from the compression of sediments, the remains of plants and animals, or the evaporation of seawater.

seismic: caused by Earth's vibrations and tremors during an earthquake.

seismic wave: an energy wave in the earth produced by an earthquake or by other means.

seismograph: an instrument that measures the intensity of a seismic wave.

seismologist: a scientist who studies seismology, the science of earthquakes and seismic waves.

shield volcano: a volcano with gently sloping sides, so it resembles a shield lying on the ground, typically built up over time by many flows of lava.

shock wave: a sharp change of pressure moving through the air caused by something moving faster than the speed of sound.

GLOSSARY

simulation: the appearance or effect of something that is used for practice.

sinkhole: a hole or depression in the land, normally caused by erosion in the underlying rock. Sinkholes can swallow cars or even homes.

species: a group of living things that are closely related and can produce young.

sporadic: happening at irregular intervals or in scattered places.

strata: a layer of material, often one of a number of parallel layers. The plural of strata is stratum.

stratovolcano: a cone-shaped volcano built up of many layers of hardened lava, pumice, and ash, also known as a composite volcano.

stress: the force applied to an object. In geology, stress is the force per unit area that is placed on a rock, which may show strain or deformation.

subduction: the sideways and downward movement of the edge of a tectonic plate beneath another plate.

submarine volcano: underwater vents or cracks in the earth's surface where magma can erupt.

subside: the gradual sinking of landforms to a lower level.

supercontinent: a large landmass, such as Pangaea, thought to have divided to form the present continents.

surface water: water that collects on the surface of the ground, such as a pond or lake.

synthetic: something made of artificial materials, using a chemical reaction.

terrain: land or ground and all of its physical features, such as hills, rocks, and water.

thermal weathering: weathering caused by temperature changes that expand and contract rock.

till: a type of sediment found under glaciers.

topography: the natural features of the land, such as mountains.

transform boundary: a boundary between tectonic plates where two plates slide alongside each other.

tsunami: a large, destructive wave caused by an earthquake.

turbine: a device that uses pressure on blades by water, air, or steam to spin generators and create electricity.

ultraviolet (UV) radiation: light with a wavelength shorter than that of visible light. UV light can cause sunburns and lead to skin cancer.

unmanned aerial vehicle (UAV): an aircraft piloted by remote control or by onboard computers, also known as a drone.

vent: a hole that lets air escape. In nature, a vent is a crack in the earth's surface that lets hot gas and lava escape, such as a volcano.

volcano: an opening in the earth's surface through which magma, ash, and gases can burst out.

volcanology: the scientific study of volcanoes.

water cycle: the movement of water from land to bodies of water, into the atmosphere, and back to the earth.

water table: the underground water supply for the planet.

weathering: destruction from rain, snow, wind, and sun.

wetland: areas where water covers or saturates the soil, such as marshes and swamps.

METRIC CONVERSIONS

Use this chart to find the metric equivalents to the English measurements in this activity. If you need to know a half measurement, divide by two. If you need to know twice the measurement, multiply by two.

ENGLISH	METRIC	
1 inch	2.5	centimeters
1 foot	30.5	centimeters
1 yard	0.9	meter
1 mile	1.6	kilometers
1 pound	0.5	kilogram
1 teaspoon	5	milliliters
1 tablespoon	15	milliliters
1 cup	237	milliliters

RESOURCES

BOOKS

Brown, Cynthia Light, and Grace Brown. *Explore Fossils! With 25 Great Projects*. Nomad Press, 2016.

Guillain, Charlotte. *The Street Beneath My Feet*. Words & Pictures, 2017.

Hutts Aston, Dianna. *A Rock Is Lively*. Chronicle Books, 2012.

Pellant, Chris. *Smithsonian Handbooks: Rocks & Minerals*. DK Smithsonian, 2002.

Reilly, Kathleen M. *Fault Lines & Tectonic Plates: Discover What Happens When the Earth's Crust Moves with 25 Projects*. Nomad Press, 2017.

Romaine, Garret. *Geology Lab for Kids: 52 Projects to Explore Rocks, Gems, Geodes, Crystals, Fossils, and Other Wonders of the Earth's Surface*. Quarry Books, 2017.

Super Earth Encyclopedia. DK Publishing, 2017.

The Rock and Gem Book: And Other Treasures of the Natural World. DK Publishing, 2016.

WEBSITES

The Incorporated Research Institutions for Seismology (IRIS):
iris.edu/hq

U.S. Geological Survey (USGS):
usgs.gov

The USGS Earthquake Hazards Program:
earthquake.usgs.gov

American Geosciences Institute (AGI):
americangeosciences.org

Oregon State University's Volcano World:
volcano.oregonstate.edu

The Volcano Information Center (VIC), University of California Santa Barbara:
volcanology.geol.ucsb.edu

British Geological Survey (BGS):
bgs.ac.uk

RESOURCES

RESOURCES

SOURCE NOTES

1 (p. 11) Gascoigne, Bamber. History World. From 2001, ongoing. http://www.historyworld.net

2 (p. 14) "History of Geology." *Prime Facts.* NSW Department of Primary Industries, 2007.
https://www.resourcesandenergy.nsw.gov.au/__data/assets/pdf_file/0005/109580/history-of-geology.pdf

3 (p. 14) Conniff, Richard. "When Continental Drift Was Considered Pseudoscience." *Smithsonian.* June 2012.
https://www.smithsonianmag.com/science-nature/when-continental-drift-was-considered-pseudoscience-90353214

4 (p. 18) Williams, Matt. "Solar System History: How Was the Earth Formed?" *Universe Today.* December 9, 2014.
https://www.universetoday.com/76509/how-was-the-earth-formed

5 (p. 22) Egger, Anne. "Defining Minerals." *Vision Learning.*
https://www.visionlearning.com/en/library/Earth-Science/6/Defining-Minerals/119

6 (p. 30) "What Is a Volcano?" NASA Space Place. https://spaceplace.nasa.gov/volcanoes2/en

7 (p. 31) "Hazardous Volcanic Events." The Volcano Information Center, University of California Santa Barbara.
http://volcanology.geol.ucsb.edu/hazards.htm

8 (p. 32 sidebar) Ewart, John W., et al. "2018 Update to the U.S. Geological Survey National Volcanic Threat Assessment:
USGS Scientific Investigations Report 2018-5140." USGS. https://pubs.er.usgs.gov/publication/sir20185140

9 (p. 35) "What Are the Benefits of Volcanoes?" *Universe Today.*
https://www.universetoday.com/32576/benefits-of-volcanoes

10 (p. 40) Zielinski, Sarah. "How to Study a Volcano." *Smithsonian.* July 28, 2011.
https://www.smithsonianmag.com/science-nature/how-to-study-a-volcano-36853465

11 (p. 49) "1906 Marked the Dawn of the Scientific Revolution." USGS Earthquake Hazards Program.
https://earthquake.usgs.gov/earthquakes/events/1906calif/18april/revolution.php

12 (p. 50) "Exploring the Earth Using Seismology." Incorporated Research Institutions for Seismology.
https://www.iris.edu/hq/inclass/fact-sheet/exploring_earth_using_seismology?zoombox=0

13 (p. 54) "Earthquake Measurement." East Asia Summit Earthquake Risk Reduction Centre.
http://nidm.gov.in/easindia2014/err/pdf/earthquake/earthquakes_measurement.pdf

14 (p. 55) "When Will it Happen Again?" USGS.
https://earthquake.usgs.gov/earthquakes/events/1906calif/18april/whenagain.php

15 (p. 66) "Weathering and Erosion." Lumen.
https://courses.lumenlearning.com/wmopen-geology/chapter/outcome-weathering-and-erosion

16 (p. 71) "Rain and Precipitation." USGS. https://water.usgs.gov/edu/earthrain.html

17 (p. 76) "What is Hydrology and What Do Hydrologists Do?" USGS. https://water.usgs.gov/edu/hydrology.html

18 (p. 78) "Components of Groundwater." Lumen.
https://courses.lumenlearning.com/wmopen-geology/chapter/outcome-components-of-groundwater

19 (p. 83) "A Short History of Energy." Union of Concerned Scientists. Feb. 6, 2014.
http://www.ucsusa.org/clean_energy/our-energy-choices/a-short-history-of-energy.html

20 (p. 88) "All about Coal." Union of Concerned Scientists.
https://www.ucsusa.org/clean-energy/coal-impacts#.XDelElxKjcs

21 (p. 90) "From the Field: Core Exercises #1." Digging the Fossil Record. The Smithsonian. May 28, 2013.
https://nmnh.typepad.com/smithsonian_fossils/2013/05/from-the-field-core-exercises-1.html

22 (p. 96) "Causes of Climate Change." NASA. http://www.ces.fau.edu/nasa/module-4/causes/sources-carbon-dioxide.php

23 (p. 105) "Global Positioning System (GPS)." Tech Target What Is.
https://searchmobilecomputing.techtarget.com/definition/Global-Positioning-System

24 (p. 106) Zimmerer, Matt. "Drones for the Geosciences." *New Mexico Earth Matters.* Volume 18, Number 1, Winter
2018. https://geoinfo.nmt.edu/publications/periodicals/earthmatters/18/n1/em_v18_n1.pdf

INDEX

INDEX